WORLD CUP

Philip Evans has written novels, one of which has a football background; and has contributed to books about football and to papers including *The Sunday Times, The Observer, Inside Football* and *World Soccer*. He becomes manic whenever Barnsley win a game, and depressive whenever they lose; wishes that people in Britain knew more about football as played overseas; and hopes that this brief book will prove to be something of a corrective.

WORLD CUP '78

PHILIP EVANS

KNIGHT BOOKS
Hodder and Stoughton

ACKNOWLEDGEMENTS

The author owes a great debt to Brian Glanville of *The Sunday Times* and John Moynihan of *The Sunday Telegraph* for having written so much good journalism about football as it is played throughout the world and for giving help whenever required; to Ernest Hecht for much good counsel, particularly about his beloved Brazil; to Leslie Vernon; to Stephen Barlay; to Jack Rollin; and his wife, Linda, for having helped to research the pictures.

For my Father

ISBN 0 340 22163 1

This edition published 1977

Printed and bound in Great Britain, for
Hodder and Stoughton Paperbacks, a division of Hodder and Stoughton Ltd, Mill Road, Dunton Green, Sevenoaks, Kent (Editorial Office: 47 Bedford Square, London, WC1 3DP)
by Cox and Wyman Ltd, London, Reading and Fakenham.

CONTENTS

PROLOGUE

Over a thousand million people watched the Final of the 1974 World Cup between West Germany and Holland; perhaps one-third of the world's population. It's a staggering statistic, that; ample testimony to the grip soccer has on the life-styles of so many people.

Of course, television has helped to spread the gospel. But the phenomenon was always there, if in an embryonic form; and is still there today, even in those countries where television is not part and parcel of the way of social life. Look at the growth and the spread of the game – and you will see a recurring pattern, of enthusiasts taking up the game on an amateur basis, of crowds going gradually to follow the sport, of the increase of professionalism that follows inevitably, of the interest in sport on the part of the media.

Here are two quotes from widely differing writers, and making very different points; but both pointing to existing evils within the game. The first is from a novel entitled *The Harder They Fall* by the American Budd Schulberg and centred on the world of professional boxing – 'An athletic sport in an atmosphere of money is like a girl from a good family in a house of ill fame.' The second is from George Orwell, who markedly disapproved of international sport. Of it he wrote – 'It is bound up with hatred, jealousy, boastfulness, disregard of all rules, and sadistic pleasure in witnessing violence – in other words, it is war minus the shooting.'

Now it is certainly true that wealth inside football has tended to introduce into it an element of greed – the media was surprised when the players at the 1974 tournament began charging 'fees' for interviews. And how many times have we watched games in which the two sides seem more intent on avoiding defeat than on actually winning? That varies from match to match, country to country, player to player. It is also true that matches between national teams (remember the war that broke out after Honduras had played a match against El Salvador –

that game ending up in riots in 1970); between teams from different countries and continents (remember the ill-fated World Club Championship) – have often degenerated into brawling, spiteful battles! It is further true that players, officials and spectators have been seriously injured – sometimes even killed – in and after the course of these games.

But the fact is that the beauty of football lies in its simplicity; that whatever the experts decide they can't change the fact that it will always be played by twenty-two persons, kicking around the pitch a piece of leather or plastic. It is this simplicity that gives it drama, that helps to highlight the particular characteristics of the players involved, that invites fanatical support and participation on the part of the people in crowds. One of the interesting things about the 1966 tournament, held in England, was the way in which the sport became alive to the people who had never seen a live match. It didn't matter whether they were Miss Flack, who lived in London or Grandmother Cuthbert who lived in Manchester – they, and millions like them, couldn't help but be caught up by the *theatre* of what they watched on television.

I don't want to sound over-naïve and ingenuous about all this, but the fact is wherever the game is played really well, people of all persuasions are prepared to make their thanksgivings – and argue against the opinions of Budd Schulberg and George Orwell. Despite learning that Johan Cruyff has just signed a new contract which will bring him the equivalent of £375,000 for a year's service to his club – F.C. Barcelona – we must say that the sport will become richer before becoming poorer.

As in everything, you have to take a wide point of view. But if the next tournament in South America throws up a handful of games that are – for the right reasons – memorable, they will serve a valuable purpose: that of reminding millions of people throughout the world that things are very much the same outside the narrow confines of our back yard.

That is the real purpose of this book – to outline the good and the bad left in the memories from the past; and to invite some understanding.

1 A LOOK AT PREVIOUS TOURNAMENTS (1930-1958)

The idea of this book is to provide a readable and interesting guide to what we all may hope to see from what will be the eleventh World Cup Final tournament to be held in South America during June 1978. But before looking at some of the teams and players who may be taking part, let us look at the past tournaments.

One reason lies in the fascination with the past and the need to recognise that the great players of the past might have been truly great – whatever their date of birth! The other reason is entirely more prosaic: that of looking at power-balances. For instance, most people readily admit that the recent teams from Brazil and West Germany have had the players and methods to most excite coaches and spectators everywhere; and we must not leave out the Holland team of the past few years. But before the war Italy won the trophy twice; and throughout the history of the tournament there have been strong teams from both Europe and South America.

We might point out at the start that 'the World Cup' was something of a misnomer; that its proper name during the years for which it was competed was 'the Jules Rimet Trophy'. The principle of an international tournament was agreed in 1920 by FIFA – Federation of International Footballing Associations – and although it was ten years before the first tournament came to be played, the guiding light behind the idea, and the man who most worked to get the tournament going was Jules Rimet, President of the French Football Federation. Thus the attractive gold trophy – won outright in 1970 by the Brazil team – came to be given his name. And the new trophy, won for the first time in 1974 by West Germany, was entitled the 'FIFA World Cup'.

A sense of history might help us to remember why the achievement of British and Irish football has often been so mediocre – when seen in international terms. The fact is that by

1930 – the year of the first tournament – the four British countries had withdrawn their associations from FIFA and were thus ineligible to compete. In 1938, it seemed the rule might be waived and, indeed, England were invited to play the rôle of guest team – once Austria had been overrun by the Nazis. But the offer was refused, and it was not until the first post-war tournament came to be played in Brazil in 1950, that any British teams took part. Even on that occasion, the seeming obstinacy and pig-headedness of the administrators had its way! The British Home International Championships preceding the Finals was recognised by FIFA as a qualifying group, in which the first *two* teams could go to Brazil (in recent years the four home countries have been very fortunate to get more than one place – the only glaring exception being that of the 1958 Final tournament: when all *four* home countries qualified!) The Scots, amazingly, decided that if they did not win the title – they would not go to Brazil! The argument is one of those nonsensical ones that ignores the large element of chance in sport – of whatever kind. The Scots lost 1-0 to England at Hampden – and like Achilles sulking in his tent, stayed at home to lick the communal wound.

But this loss of twenty years – playing against the opposition with the will to win – was something badly missed by the four countries. If Britain gave modern football to the world then the world soon caught up with, and overtook, us in terms of skill, ball-control and tactics. Internationals played as 'friendlies' were all very well but who can forget the way England players – including Finney and Matthews – were received when they returned from Brazil in 1950 – where they had ignominiously been defeated by a team from the U.S.A.? And the lessons they were shown three years later by the brilliant teams who came from Hungary. Let alone the failure of England to qualify for the Final tournament of 1974!

We have to face the fact that – as in many things – the pupil has begun to outstrip the master; and forced him to get back to basic principles himself. I believe that sport – as most things – goes round in cycles, and that if it is any country's turn to get back and brush up the basic techniques – those will stand them in good stead in years to come. In this book, I've tried to cut down to a minimum the material about pre-war tournaments – those to which the four countries who play in the Home International Competition sent no teams.

World Cup 1930 – held in Uruguay

Not unnaturally the first tournament was a strange affair. Travel to Uruguay from Europe at the time was costly and time-consuming. Little wonder then that so many of the European competitors withdrew – Italy, Spain, Austria, Hungary, Germany, Switzerland and Czechoslovakia among them. In many ways one of the stars of the show proved to be King Carol of Rumania – he not only picked the Rumanian team, but ensured that the players were given adequate time off from their firms. With only France, Belgium and Yugoslavia of the other European countries being involved, the affair was set for a South American victory.

Why Uruguay as the place to hold a tournament such as this? It seems strange; but the fact is that the Uruguayans had taken the Olympic titles both in 1924 and 1928, they had promised to build a handsome new stadium in which the games could be played and had further guaranteed the expenses of all the competing teams.

Thirteen countries competed in four pools, the winners of each pool moving to the semi-final stage, together with the final played on a knock-out basis.

When it came to it, two of the semi-finalists could be ranked as surprises, one as a complete surprise. That was the United States, for so long the chopping-block for skilful South American teams in Olympic competition, but now able to use some formidable ex-British professionals. In their first game the Americans tanned Belgium 3-0; then beat Paraguay by the same score and qualified for the semi-finals where they would meet Argentina.

The Argentinians themselves had won their group without dropping a point, and the other semi-finalists were Yugoslavia – winners by 2-1 over Brazil and 4-0 over Bolivia; and the host team, Uruguay who scratched and scraped to find their form before going through against Peru 1-0 and then took the Rumanians to the cleaners by four goals to none. The stage was set for the South Americans to face the invaders.

In the event, the semi-finals were an anti-climax. Against a skilful and ruthless Argentinian team, the strength and brawn of the United States team proved ineffective – they went down by six goals to one. And in the other game, the Uruguayans thrashed Yugoslavia by the same score.

Both victorious teams were undoubtedly strong. The Uruguayans had prepared for the tournament with a dedication that has recently been commonplace, then considered extraordinary, one that made nonsense of any thought that they were still amateurs. For two celibate months the players had been trained ruthlessly, deprived of freedom, a rigorous curfew imposed on their nocturnal wanderings. When their brilliant goalkeeper, Mazzali, was discovered late one night, shoes in hand, sneaking in after a night on the town he was thrown out and his place given to a reserve.

There has never been much love lost between South American teams on the football field, and the natural rivalry that already existed between Uruguay and Argentina had recently been pointed by the defeat of the latter at the hands of the former in the final of the 1928 Olympic tournament.

The Final, strangely, was played in a comparatively peaceful way, the Uruguayans winning by four goals to two after having trailed by the odd goal in three at half-time. Off the field and after the game came the expected Argentinian protests – that the Uruguayans had been 'brutal', that the referee had been bought. Relations between the footballing authorities of the two countries were broken off. But the first World Cup had been played – and won handsomely by a very good team.

1930 – Final Stages

Semi-Finals

ARGENTINA 6, UNITED STATES 1 (1-0)

ARGENTINA: Botasso; Della Torre, Paternoster; Evaristo, J., Monti, Orlandini; Peucelle, Scopelli, Stabile, Ferreira (capt.), Evaristo, M.
USA: Douglas; Wood, Moorhouse; Gallacher, Tracey, Auld; Brown, Gonsalvez, Patenaude, Florie (capt.), McGhee.
SCORERS: Monti, Scopelli, Stabile (2), Peucelle (2) for Argentina; Brown for USA.

URUGUAY 6, YUGOSLAVIA 1 (3-1)

URUGUAY: Ballesteros; Nasazzi (capt.), Mascheroni; Andrade, Fernandez, Gestido; Dorado, Scarone, Anselmo, Cea, Iriarte.
YUGOSLAVIA: Yavocic; Ivkovic (capt.), Mihailovic; Arsenievic, Stefanovic, Djokic; Tirnanic, Marianovic, Beck, Vujadinovic, Seculic.
SCORERS: Cea (3), Anselmo (2), Iriarte for Uruguay; Seculic for Yugoslavia.

Final

URUGUAY 4, ARGENTINA 2 (1-2)

URUGUAY: Ballesteros; Nasazzi (capt.), Mascheroni; Andrade, Fernandez, Gestido; Dorado, Scarone, Castro, Cea, Iriarte.
ARGENTINA: Botasso; Della Torre, Paternoster; Evaristo, J., Monti, Suarez; Peucelle, Varallo, Stabile, Ferreira (capt.), Evaristo, M.
SCORERS: Dorado, Cea, Iriarte, Castro for Uruguay; Peucelle, Stabile for Argentina.

World Cup 1934 – held in Italy

Four years later, the competition was altogether more representative and better attended. The Uruguayans stayed away – piqued by the refusal of so many European teams to grace their tournament in 1930; and the Argentinians, having lost too many of their star players to Italian clubs, came with something of a reserve side. More important was the background to the tournament, played in Fascist Italy. Mussolini's features stared up from the official booklets, stared down from the Tribune of Honour in the various stadia.

In the event, the Italians had a fine team, pulled together by Vittorio Pozzo, a remarkable manager. It contained three Argentinians of supposed Italian extraction – the fearsome Monti among them. They were included on the justification that if they were eligible to do military service for Italy, they were eligible to play football for Italy. From the start Pozzo proved himself a master psychologist – and he needed to be. He was dealing with temperamental stars of great technical ability in individual terms, with little will to play with and for each other. Pozzo it was who welded together a squad of seeming disparates by locking the players up *in ritiro*, forcing them to live and train closely together, matching the prima donna antics of the one against those of the other, until all came to feel that they were being treated equally. Although the strong Austrian *wunderteam* was there, although Hungary and Spain could be fancied, many things pointed towards a second victory in the tournament for the team playing at 'home'.

In fact, there were several organisational changes from the first tournament. Whereas all the games in Uruguay had been played in the new stadium, purpose-built in Montevideo, it had been realised that in future more than one city would be needed to accommodate all the games. In Uruguay, thirteen teams had competed; here there were sixteen, this complete turnout allowing a change in the formula so that the tournament was a knock-out affair from first to last; and the cities that were graced by first-round ties were eight – Rome, Naples, Florence, Milan, Turin, Bologna, Genoa and Trieste.

The gallant Americans were there, ready to prove that their performance in 1930 had been no flash in the pan; but they met Italy in the first round and lost by seven goals to one. Spain, with the fabulous Zamora in goal, beat Brazil 3-1; the Germans, another team not to be under-valued, beat Belgium 5-2; Austria scraped through against France by the odd goal in five and after extra time; and Hungary revenged the bitter humiliation of having lost to Egypt in the 1924 Olympiad. On to the second round, with Italy and Spain drawn against each other.

Zamora was much feared, a goalkeeper who in the past had too often barred the way of Italian forwards not to be taken seriously, even at his current age of thirty-three. In the event he played a superb game, plucking centres and corner-kicks out of the air with sure timing and adhesive hands. But his courage had a price to be paid. Although he withstood 120 minutes of pressure as the game – stymied at 1-1 – moved into extra time, there seemed little chance at the final whistle that he would be fit to play the next day when the replay was due to take place.

Nor did he. And although the Spanish held Italy to just the one goal, they had been forced to field five other reserves. When played, the second game was even more pathetically refereed, so badly that the Swiss official concerned was suspended by his own federation. The Italians were through, but with that smear of luck that successful teams will always need to make their point.

To join them in the semi-finals came Germany – well organised in defence, and fortunate that the Swedes were down to ten men for much of their 2-1 victory; Austria, who beat Hungary by the same score in a brawling game that could never have suited the Austrians' penchant for swift, close passing; and Czechoslovakia, who came through against Switzerland 3-2.

That left Italy to face the fancied Austrians only two days after that bruising replay against Spain, and though there was only the one goal in their favour, their command was seldom in question. The Austrians were forced to wait until the forty-second minute before even aiming a shot at goal.

In the Final, the Italians came face to face with Czechoslovakia, much too clever for the Germans in the previous round, and were given a real run for their money. The Czechs took the lead through Puc in the middle of the second half, soon after missed two golden chances and hit a post. You shouldn't be allowed such freedom in competition, and much to their dismay the Czechs found Italy equalising with only eight minutes to go – a freak goal from Orsi, struck with his right foot and curling wickedly in the air. (The following day in practice, he tried twenty times – without success – to repeat it.) In the seventh minute of extra time, the Italians scored the winning goal through Schiavio and that was that – victory snatched from the enterprising Czechs just when they seemed to have the thing in the bag.

Neutral experts were eager to make their points. The advantage of home ground, they pointed out, had been decisive (it always is, surely); the frenzied, para-military support; the consequent intimidation of referees – these all may have been decisive. They may, but no one doubted that the 'World Cup' was now firmly established, on the road to improvement in terms of organisation and skill.

1934 – Final Stages

Semi-Finals

CZECHOSLOVAKIA 3, GERMANY 1 (1-0). *Rome*

CZECHOSLOVAKIA: Planika (capt.); Burger, Ctyroky; Kostalek, Cambal, Krcil; Junek, Svoboda, Sobotka, Nejedly, Puc.
GERMANY: Kress; Haringer, Busch; Zielinski, Szepan (capt.), Bender; Lehner, Siffling, Conen, Noack, Kobierski.
SCORERS: Nejedly (2), Krcil for Czechoslovakia; Noack for Germany.

ITALY 1, AUSTRIA 0 (1-0). *Milan*

ITALY: Combi (capt.); Monzeglio, Allemandi; Ferraris IV, Monti, Bertolini; Guaita, Meazza, Schiavio, Ferrari, Orsi.
AUSTRIA: Platzer; Cisar, Sesztar; Wagner, Smistik (capt.), Urbanek; Zischek, Bican, Sindelar, Schall, Viertel.
SCORER: Guaita for Italy.

Third Place Match

GERMANY 3, AUSTRIA 2 (3-1). *Naples*

GERMANY: Jakob; Janes, Busch; Zielinski, Muensenberg, Bender; Lehner, Siffling, Conen, Szepan (capt.), Heidemann.
AUSTRIA: Platzer; Cisar, Sesztar; Wagner, Smistik (capt.), Urbanek; Zischek, Braun, Bican, Horwath, Viertel.
SCORERS: Lehner (2), Conen for Germany; Horwath, Seszta for Austria.

Final

ITALY 2, CZECHOSLOVAKIA 1 (0-0) (1-1) after extra time. *Rome*

ITALY: Combi (capt.); Monzeglio, Allemandi; Ferraris IV, Monti, Bertolini; Guiata, Meazza, Schiavio, Ferrari, Orsi.
CZECHOSLOVAKIA: Planika (capt.); Zenisek, Ctyroky; Kostalek, Cambal, Krcil; Junek, Svoboda, Sobotka, Nejedly, Puc.
SCORERS: Orsi, Schiavio for Italy; Puc for Czechoslovakia.

World Cup 1938 – held in France

Again the tournament was played in several venues, again it was played along strictly knock-out lines, again it was won by Italy. And won more convincingly, it must be said. As if to prove that their football was the best in the world, the Italians had entered for, and won, the 1936 Olympiad – aided by the use of dubious 'amateurs', aided by the unpleasant Nazi ambience; but still a further victory to point to, further evidence that they had emerged as a powerful side.

Pozzo was still at the helm; to join Meazza in the forward line was Silvio Piola – a tall, powerful centre-forward who would score so many goals in Italian league football and for the international team; in place of the uncompromising Monti, Pozzo had at his disposal another South American hatchet-man in Andreolo of Uruguay; and to replace Combi in goal was yet another excellent keeper in Olivieri.

If victory in 1934 had been important to the Italians as a propaganda weapon, success in 1938 was deemed no less important and for the same reason. Political interest reared its head elsewhere. The Argentinians refused to come because they had not been given the competition; Spain was forced to withdraw on account of the bloody Civil War; and the Austrians – their country having been swallowed up by the Nazis – found themselves without a team for which to play. In fact, the 'German' team comprised seven players from Germany, four from Austria.

The first game went to 1-1; the replay panned out to a Swiss victory by four goals to two. Trailing by the odd goal in three into the second half, all seemed lost to the Swiss when they lost a player through injury. Not a bit of it. They waited for his return, equalised soon after, and then ran through for two more goals.

There were other surprises in store, given the context of history. The Dutch East Indies took part – annihilated by a formidable Hungarian side 6-0; and Cuba played well enough – beating the Rumanians after a replay in the first round – for us to wonder what has happened to Cuban football in the last three decades. Italy made heavy weather of Norway, winning by the odd goal in three after extra time; and in an extraordinary game, again needing extra time to decide the outcome, the Brazilians beat Poland 6-5. Playing at centre-forward for the South Americans that day – and scorer, like the Pole, Willimowski, of four goals – was Leonidas, the Black Diamond, a player of extraordinary reflex and lightning anticipation. On to the second round.

The Cubans came a great cropper at the hands of Sweden, losing 8-0; the Hungarians, with the mercurial Sarosi at centre-forward, put out gallant Switzerland 2-0; the Italians, their morale revived by the cunning Pozzo, and thanks to two goals from Piola, beat France 3-1; and the fireworks were reserved for the game between the Brazilians and the Czechs.

It was nothing less than a holocaust, with three players – two of them Brazilians – sent off, and two more retiring to hospital with broken limbs. Not for nothing was the game to be known as the 'Battle of Bordeaux', not for the last time was the tension of a great occasion to prove too much for the Brazilians. They ran out of spirit in the second half, after Leonidas had given them the lead, gave away a penalty and the world rubbed its hands or shielded its eyes in expectation of the replay.

In the event, the affair was peaceful, mild to an amazing degree. The Brazilians made nine changes, the Czechs six; Leonidas scored yet again, equalising the opening goal from the Czechs, and Roberto it was who tucked away the winner.

And then came even more crazy an episode. Drawn against the Italians, the Brazilian team manager announced that Leonidas and Tim – his two great goal-scorers – would miss the semi-final round and were being 'kept for the final'. Nobody believed him, of course; but when the teams ran on to the pitch – no Leonidas, no Tim. *Hamlet* without the Prince and Horatio indeed; and playing straight into the hands of the Italians. They scored the first two of the three goals in the game, were seldom under hard pressure.

In the other semi-final Sweden scored a goal within the first thirty-five seconds of play, then crumpled before the vaunted Hungarian attack, who scored five times, thrice before half-time. So dominant was the play of the central Europeans that for much of the second half a large blackbird sat peacefully on the field of play twenty yards away from the Hungarian goalkeeper.

Italy against Hungary in the Final, then; but first the play-off for third place, and the salt really rubbed into Brazilian wounds. Leonidas returned and scored two goals in a 4-2 victory over Sweden, posing questions that might have overtaxed the Italian defence had he ever been given the chance to ask them of it, and running out as the tournament's top scorer.

The Final itself seemed to be symbolised by the struggle between two great centre-forwards; Piola for Italy, Sarosi for Hungary. For all the skill of the latter, it was the bite and drive of the former that proved decisive. Two early goals within a minute provided a dramatic beginning; then the bustling style of the Italians took them into a two-goal lead. Hungary came back with twenty minutes to go through Sarosi, threatened briefly, then went under finally with ten minutes to play when Piola drove in the Italians' fourth goal.

Italy had unquestionably deserved her triumph this time. And the World Cup would remain in Italian hands for twelve long years while the world went to war and many players of talent died violent deaths.

1938 – Final Stages

Semi-Finals

ITALY 2, BRAZIL 1 (2-0). *Marseilles*

ITALY: Olivieri; Foni, Rava; Serantoni, Andreolo, Locatelli; Biavati, Meazza (capt.), Piola, Ferrari, Colaussi.
BRAZIL: Walter; Domingas Da Guia, Machados; Zeze, Martin (capt.), Alfonsinho; Lopex, Luisinho, Peracio, Romeo, Patesko.
SCORERS: Colaussi, Meazza (penalty) for Italy; Romeo for Brazil.

HUNGARY 5, SWEDEN 1 (3-1). *Paris, Colombes*

HUNGARY: Szabo; Koranyi, Biro; Szalay, Turai, Lazar; Sas, Szengeller, Sarosi (capt.), Toldi, Titkos.
SWEDEN: Abrahamson; Eriksson, Kjellgren; Almgren, Jacobsson, Svanstroem; Wetterstroem, Keller (capt.), Andersson H., Jonasson, Nyberg.
SCORERS: Szengeller (3), Titkos, Sarosi for Hungary; Nyberg for Sweden.

Third Place Match

BRAZIL 4, SWEDEN 2 (1-2). *Bordeaux*

BRAZIL: Batatoes; Domingas Da Guia, Machados; Zeze, Brandao, Alfonsinho; Roberto, Romeo, Leonidas (capt.), Peracio, Patesko.
SWEDEN: Abrahamson; Eriksson, Nilssen; Almgren, Linderholm, Svanstroem (capt.); Berssen, Andersson H., Jonasson, Andersson, A., Nyberg.
SCORERS: Jonasson, Nyberg for Sweden; Romeo, Leonidas (2), Peracio for Brazil.

Final

ITALY 4, HUNGARY 2 (3-1). *Paris, Colombes*

ITALY: Olivieri; Foni, Rava; Serantoni, Andreolo, Locatelli; Biavati, Meazza (capt.), Piola, Ferrari, Colaussi.
HUNGARY: Szabo; Polgar, Biro; Szalay, Szucs, Lazar; Sas, Vincze, Sarosi (capt.), Szengeller, Titkos.
SCORERS: Colaussi (2), Piola (2) for Italy; Titkos, Sarosi for Hungary.

World Cup 1950 – held in Brazil

Twenty years had elapsed since the tournament was last held in South America, and the problems thrown up had not, it appeared, been diluted. Thirteen teams had competed in 1930, the tally in 1950 would be no larger. The Indians qualified, but would not come; Scotland, as we have seen, fatuously stayed out; the Austrians were going through one of their frequent bouts of diffidence, and felt their team not strong enough (even though they had just beaten Italy – who would play); Hungary, like the Russians, remained in Cold War isolation; the French, knocked out in their qualifying group, and then reprieved, felt the journey too long and arduous; and the Argentinians had squabbled with the Brazilian Federation. As for West Germany, they were still barred from FIFA.

Thirteen teams, then; and the gaps made nonsense of the new pool system, which would apply not merely to the four qualifying groups, but also to the final group – competed in by the four winners. The Uruguayans, for example, had only to play one jog-trot of a game to be through to the final pool – a victory by eight goals to none over Bolivia. Little wonder that they seemed more fresh and zestful in the late stages of the tournament.

The massive Maracana stadium in Rio de Janeiro was still being built when the tournament started – and when it finished. Brazil featured there in the opening match, beating Mexico by four clear goals in front of a happily partisan crowd of 155,000 (the Maracana would hold 200,000). Two of their goals came from Ademir – yet another of those incredible ball-playing inside forwards that the Brazilians had a penchant for producing. Like the Uruguayans in 1930, the Italians in 1934, the Brazilians had prepared with military thoroughness – an air of celibacy and special diets reigned supreme. They would qualify for the final pool – but not before drawing against Switzerland with a mis-chosen team, and having to fight hard against a Yugoslavian side.

Co-favourites with Brazil were – England! Appearing for the first time in the competition, with some devastating form behind them, the English had to be fancied. Whatever the balance of power suggested, eyes turned interestedly towards them. They had yet to find a centre-forward to replace Lawton, but Matthews was there, Finney was there, Mortensen was there, Mannion was there; and these were players whose skill was legendary. They scraped through their first game against Chile, finding the heat and humidity so oppressive that they took oxygen at half-time. And then came the shock of the tournament – possibly one of the greatest shocks in the history of international football – as England went down by just the one goal to the United States.

A number of the American players had stayed up into the early hours of the morning; several of them expected a cricket score, and indicated as much to British journalists. In the event, it was eight minutes before half-time when Gaetjens headed in Bahr's cross (or was it a miskicked shot?); and that, whatever the English forwards would do in the second half, remained the only goal of the match. The victory of Chile over the Americans a few days later and by five goals to two emphasised England's shame. And although Matthews and Milburn were brought in for the final English game against Spain, although many felt the English deserved at least a draw, the die was cast. England were out of a tournament whose previous editions they had ignored, one for which they had been heavily favoured.

Into the final pool along with Spain, Brazil and Uruguay went Sweden. They had won the 1948 Olympic tournament with a team that included Gren, Nordhal and Liedholm – all, alas, now playing in Italy and blocked from selection. What irony, then, that in their first game the Swedes should play the Italians and win by the odd goal in five! A draw against the other team in their pool, Paraguay, and Sweden were through.

Little good it was to do them, with Brazil now turning on all the fireworks. In their first game the Brazilians beat Sweden 7-1; in their second, Spain by 6-1. Their trio of inside forwards – Jair, Ademir and Zizinho – seemed uncontrollable: professional counterparts of those countless boys who juggle footballs on the Copacabana beach from sunrise to sunset. Brazil, it seemed, would handsomely win the title.

The challenge came from Uruguay, held to a draw by Spain, victors over Sweden (who would in turn defeat the Spanish with that perverse logic that accompanies these affairs). If the Brazilians had Jair, Ademir and Zizinho – the Uruguayans had Juan Schiaffino, as thin as a piece of paper, a player of enormous technical skills that would later be appreciated by European audiences when he found his way into the cauldron of Italian league football, once described by Tommy Docherty (until recently manager of Manchester United) as the best player he ever had to face.

But for all Schiaffino's skills, the Uruguayans were the first to admit that they were unable to match the Brazilians in terms of pure technique. Tactical expertise was needed, and tactical expertise was used. Hard as they might try, the Brazilian forwards seldom seemed able to penetrate the light-blue defensive barrier thrown up by the Uruguayan defence, the dark mastery of Maspoli in the opposing goal. No score at half-time.

Two minutes after the interval, the Maracana erupted as Friaça closed in from the wing, shot – and scored. But the Uruguayans had made their point, knew that they were able to cope with the 'superteam' that opposed them. Schiaffino it was who put them ahead, ghosting through the centre to knock in a cross. And ten minutes before the end, Ghiggia, the Uruguayan left-wing, cut in, beat his fullback to score.

The 'right team' had lost; Uruguay had won a match of breath-taking quality and the tournament for a second time after an interval of twenty years.

1950 – Final Stages

Final Pool

URUGUAY 2, SPAIN 2 (1-2). *São Paulo*

URUGUAY: Maspoli; Gonzales, M., Tejera; Gonzales, W., Varela (capt.), Andrade; Ghiggia, Perez, Miguez, Schiaffino, Vidal.
SPAIN: Ramallets; Alonzo, Gonzalvo II; Gonzalvo III, Parra, Puchades; Basora, Igoa, Zarra, Molowny, Gainza.
SCORERS: Ghiggia, Varela for Uruguay; Basora (2) for Spain.

BRAZIL 7, SWEDEN 1 (3-1). *Rio*

BRAZIL: Barbosa; Augusto (capt.), Juvenal; Bauer, Danilo, Bigode; Maneca, Zizinho, Ademir, Jair, Chico.
SWEDEN: Svensson; Samuelsson, Nilsson, E.; Andersson, Nordahl, K., Gard; Sundqvist, Palmer, Jeppson, Skoglund, Nilsson, S.
SCORERS: Ademir (4), Chico (2), Maneca for Brazil; Andersson (penalty) for Sweden.

URUGUAY 3, SWEDEN 2 (1-2). *São Paulo*

URUGUAY: Paz; Gonzales, M., Tejera; Gambetta, Varela (capt.), Andrade; Ghiggia, Perez, Miguez, Schiaffino, Vidal.
SWEDEN: Svensson; Samuelsson, Nilsson, E.; Andersson, Johansson, Gard; Johnsson, Palmer, Melberg, Skoglund, Sundqvist.
SCORERS: Palmer, Sundqvist for Sweden; Ghiggia, Miguez (2) for Uruguay.

BRAZIL 6, SPAIN 1 (3-0). *Rio*

BRAZIL: Barbosa; Augusto (capt.), Juvenal; Bauer, Danilo, Bigode; Friaça, Zizinho, Ademir, Jair, Chico.

Spain: Eizaguirre; Alonzo, Gonzalvo II; Gonzalvo III, Parra, Puchades; Basora, Igoa, Zarra, Panizo, Gainza.
Scorers: Jair (2), Chico (2), Zizinho, Parra (own goal) for Brazil; Igoa for Spain.

SWEDEN 3, SPAIN 1 (2-0). *São Paulo*

Sweden: Svensson; Samuelsson, Nilsson, E.; Andersson, Johansson, Gard; Sundqvist, Mellberg, Rydell, Palmer, Johnsson.
Spain: Eizaguirre; Asensi, Alonzo; Silva, Parra, Puchades; Basora, Fernandez, Zarra, Panizo, Juncosa.
Scorers: Johansson, Mellberg, Palmer for Sweden; Zarra for Spain.

URUGUAY 2, BRAZIL 1 (0-0). *Rio*

Uruguay: Maspoli; Gonzales, M., Tejera; Gambetta, Varela (capt.), Andrade; Ghiggia, Perez, Miguez, Schiaffino, Moran.
Brazil: Barbosa; Augusto (capt.), Juvenal; Bauer, Danilo, Bigode; Friaça, Zizinho, Ademir, Jair, Chico.
Scorers: Friaça for Brazil; Schiaffino, Ghiggia for Uruguay.

Final Positions

					Goals		
	P	W	D	L	F	A	Pts
Uruguay	3	2	1	0	7	5	5
Brazil	3	2	0	1	14	4	4
Sweden	3	1	0	2	6	11	2
Spain	3	0	1	2	4	11	1

World Cup 1954 – held in Switzerland

And here was another instance of the 'wrong' team coming through to take the trophy, when Germany won their first World Cup and the brilliant Hungarians were denied their right. Bizarre organisation in which two teams from each group were 'seeded', leaving the supposedly stronger teams apart in the early stages; and the presence of a handful of really formidable teams in Hungary, Brazil, Germany, Uruguay and Austria – both these ensured that in later years this would come to be known as the last of the 'open' tournaments, the last in which teams seemed more concerned to score, than to prevent, goals.

England were there, shaky after a hammering administered at the hands of the Hungarians only a couple of weeks earlier when their winter defeat at Wembley had been exposed as no fluke. In Budapest they lost 7-1, a disorganised rabble in front of brilliant passing and shooting. History was on their side, Matthews, Wright and Finney in it; but few gave them any chance. And Scotland were also there – having repeated one part of their rôle from 1950 by losing to England; this time, however, having the courage to enter in spite of their lack of confidence.

Uruguay were strong, entering their first European tournament, unbeaten to date. Schiaffino was still there; they had splendid new wingers in Abbadie and Borges; a powerful stopper in Santamaria, later to be the bulwark of Real Madrid's invincible side. The Brazilians were slightly fancied despite being involved in a period of neurotic assessment. Their game, they felt, was too ingenious; so they closed the defence with care, came down hard on flair unless it could be harnessed to teamwork. They would wait until 1958 before perfecting the balance, but in their first game of the tournament – a 5-0 drubbing of Mexico – they introduced two great backs in the Santoses (no relation), a fine distributor in Didì, a unique winger in Julinho –

a man of violent pace, superb balance, close control and with a rocket of a shot.

In *their* first game, the Uruguayans beat the Czechs 2-0; then annihilated Scotland by seven clear goals, Borges and Abbadie getting five between them. The Scottish campaign had not been helped by dissension off the pitch and the resignation, after the first defeat at the hands of Austria, of Andy Beattie, the team manager; but the Uruguayans looked good, Schiaffino in regal form. Through to join them in the quarter-finals went Yugoslavia – who had held Brazil to a 1-1 draw in a memorable match in which their goalkeeper Beara (a former ballet dancer) had performed prodigies in defence and Zebec had given evidence of his all-round skill; England, drawing 4-4 with Belgium first time out before beating Switzerland 2-0; the Swiss, thanks to a played-off game against the Italians, who had been strangely static; Brazil; Austria, who defeated the Czechs 5-0 with their talented half-back Ocwirk emerging as one of the players of the tournament; Germany and Hungary.

This last pair provided most of the news. The Hungarians went out in their first game, drubbed Korea 9-0; then were forced to play the Germans, the latter not having been seeded. The wily German coach, Sepp Herberger, cleverly decided to throw away this match, banked on winning the play-off against Turkey (which he did) and fielded a team largely composed of reserves. The Hungarians came through 8-3, the Germans had not given away any secrets; but most important, it was in this game that Puskas was injured, that a vital part of the Hungarian machine was put out of action.

The Hungarians had won the 1952 Olympiad; in Hidegkuti they had a deep-lying centre-forward of great verve and authority, a man who could make and score brilliant goals; at inside forward they had Kocsis and Puskas, the former a little man with the neck of a bull who could leap great heights to head a ball, the latter with a hammer of a left foot; and in the half-back line they had an excellent exemplar in Boszik, always driving forward with speed, ingenuity and strength. With four players of genius and others who were little behind, it was easy to see why the Hungarians were widely considered favourites to win the tournament.

Two things upset them. First, the injury to Puskas, who would play again only in the Final and at half-speed. The other was what came to be known as the 'Battle of Berne', a disgraceful quarter-final tie which pitted them against the Brazilians. Hungary won the game 4-2 after being two up in the first eight minutes, after giving away a penalty, after themselves scoring from one, after Nilton Santos and Boszik had been sent off for fighting in a match that seemed more suited to a boxing ring. After the game the Brazilians invaded the Hungarian dressing-room, went berserk and came close to inflicting further serious injury on the Hungarian players. Hungary were through to the semi-finals where they would play an unforgettable game against Uruguay, victors over an England team that fought hard, laid siege to the Uruguayan goal without really capitalising on their approach play (where Matthews was outstanding) and was let down by Merrick, the goalkeeper.

The other semi-final would be between Austria who beat Switzerland 7-5 after having trailed 2-4 at half-time; and Germany, ploughing on with force and thoroughness against the talented Yugoslavs. In the event, the Germans 'came good' when it mattered. They scored twice from penalties in their 6-1 win, now seemed ominously hard to beat.

The Hungary–Uruguay game, even without Puskas, was a gem. Two-nil up with fifteen minutes to go, the Hungarians seemed through – until the Uruguayans counter-attacked. Schiaffino put Hohberg through, the move was repeated three minutes before the end, and extra time was on. It nearly began without Hohberg himself, who had been forced to retire 'injured' after having been overwhelmed by delighted team mates. But recover he did, to burst through early in the first period of extra time and smack in a shot – that came back off a post. In retrospect, it can be seen as the turning point; for Kocsis twice in the second period rose to head home crosses; and Hungary were through.

A Puskas far from fit, too chubby round the middle and with a sore ankle, returned for the Final. Great player though he was, the Hungarians had managed well without him, and might have done better to discard him (as Alf Ramsey would prefer Roger Hunt to Jimmy Greaves twelve years later, sacrificing rare gifts to teamwork, and win). Yet again, the Hungarians went off like a train, two goals up in eight minutes, seemingly well on the way to a victory that awaited them.

What mattered most, perhaps, was the swiftness of the German reply. Three minutes later they had drawn back a goal through Morlock; then Rahn drove home a corner; at the other end Turek remained in stupendous form between the goalposts; Rahn got the goal that would be the winner; Puskas scored – only to be given offside; and the invincible Hungarians had been beaten.

They had been beaten by a better team on the day; by the punishment of earlier games against South Americans; by a certain amount of internal dissension to do with the injury to Puskas. Yet they remained the best team that Europe had seen to date, possibly the best team that Europe has yet seen. And it took an almost equally brilliant team from the other side of the world and four years later, to push them into the light shadows; the amazing Brazilians of the Sweden tournament, and their latest wonder-boy – Pelé.

1954 – Final Stages

Quarter-Finals

GERMANY 2, YUGOSLAVIA 0 (1-0). *Geneva*

GERMANY: Turek; Laband, Kohlmeyer; Eckel, Liebrich, Mai; Rahn, Morlock, Walter, O., Walter, F. (capt.), Schaefer.
YUGOSLAVIA: Beara; Stankovic, Crnkovic; Cjaicowski I, Horvat, Boskov; Milutinovic, Mitic (capt.), Vukas, Bobek, Zebec.
SCORERS: Horvat (own goal), Rahn for Germany.

HUNGARY 4, BRAZIL 2 (2-1). *Berne*

HUNGARY: Grosics; Buzansky, Lantos; Boszik (capt.), Lorant, Zakarias; Toth, M., Kocsis, Hidegkuti, Czibor, Toth, J.
BRAZIL: Castilho; Santos, D., Santos, N.; Brandaozinho, Pinheiro (capt.), Bauer; Julinho, Didì, Indio, Tozzi, Maurinho.
SCORERS: Hidegkuti (2), Kocsis, Lantos (penalty) for Hungary; Santos, D. (penalty), Julinho for Brazil.

AUSTRIA 7, SWITZERLAND 5 (2-4). *Lausanne*

AUSTRIA: Schmied; Hanappi, Barschandt; Ocwirk (capt.), Happel, Koller; Koerner, R., Wagner, Stojaspal, Probst, Koerner, A.
SWITZERLAND: Parlier; Neury, Kernen; Eggimann, Bocquet (capt.), Casali; Antenen, Vonlanthen, Hugi, Ballaman, Fatton.
SCORERS: Ballaman (2), Hugi (2), Hanappi (own goal) for Switzerland; Koerner, A. (2), Ocwirk, Wagner (3), Probst for Austria.

URUGUAY 4, ENGLAND 2 (2-1). *Basel*

URUGUAY: Maspoli; Santamaria, Martinez; Andrade, Varela (capt.), Cruz; Abbadie, Ambrois, Miguez, Schiaffino, Borges.
ENGLAND: Merrick; Staniforth, Byrne; McGarry, Wright (capt.), Dickinson; Matthews, Broadis, Lofthouse, Wilshaw, Finney.
SCORERS: Borges, Varela, Schiaffino, Ambrois for Uruguay; Lofthouse, Finney for England.

Semi-Finals

GERMANY 6, AUSTRIA 1 (1-0). *Basel*

GERMANY: Turek; Posipal, Kohlmeyer; Eckel, Liebrich, Mai; Rahn, Morlock, Walter, O., Walter, F. (capt.), Schaefer.
AUSTRIA: Zeman; Hanappi, Schleger; Ocwirk (capt.), Happel, Koller; Koerner, R., Wagner, Stojaspal, Probst, Koerner, A.

SCORERS: Schaefer, Morlock, Walter, F. (2 penalties), Walter, O. (2) for Germany; Probst for Austria.

HUNGARY 4, URUGUAY 2 (1-0) (2-2) after extra time. *Lausanne*

HUNGARY: Grosics; Buzansky, Lantos; Bostik (capt.), Lorant, Zakarias; Budai, Kocsis, Palotas, Hidegkuti, Czibor.
URUGUAY: Maspoli; Santamaria, Martinez; Andrade (capt.), Carballo, Cruz; Souto, Ambrois, Schiaffino, Hohberg, Borges.
SCORERS: Czibor, Hidegkuti, Kocsis (2) for Hungary; Hohberg (2) for Uruguay.

Third Place Match

AUSTRIA 3, URUGUAY 1 (1-1). *Zurich*

AUSTRIA: Schmied; Hanappi, Barschandt; Ocwirk (capt.), Kollman, Koller; Koener, R., Wagner, Dienst, Stojaspal, Probst.
URUGUAY: Maspoli; Santamaria, Martinez; Andrade (capt.), Carballo, Cruz; Abbadie, Hohberg, Mendez, Schiaffino, Borges.
SCORERS: Stojaspal (penalty), Cruz (own goal), Ocwirk for Austria; Hohberg for Uruguay.

Final

GERMANY 3, HUNGARY 2 (2-2). *Berne*

GERMANY: Turek; Posipal, Kohlmeyer; Eckel, Liebrich, Mai; Rahn, Morlock, Walter, O., Walter, F. (capt.), Schaefer.
HUNGARY: Grosics; Buzansky, Lantos; Boszik, Lorant (capt.), Zakarias; Czibor, Kocsis, Hidegkuti, Puskas, Toth, J.
SCORERS: Puskas, Czibor for Hungary; Morlock, Rahn (2) for Germany.

World Cup 1958 – held in Sweden

The Brazilians came and conquered – came to Sweden as one of the favourites (thanks to the on-paper banality of much of the opposition), conquered with an extraordinary demonstration of prowess and skill in the Final. The backstage people concerned, for the first time, harnessed the natural talent of the players, made the team's play really effective. In 1950 the players had been allowed to express themselves too freely; in 1954, they had been too restrained. Now the blend was right.

Yet the truth remains, that like the Hungarians before them but to a lesser degree, the Brazilians proved that great teams – so called – depend essentially upon the coming-together in one period of time of a clutch of great players. Didì was in evidence again, full of lithe passes, famous for his 'falling leaf' shot – struck with the outside of the foot and fading distressingly in mid-flight; the Santoses were playing still at fullback; and in the forward line were two new geniuses in Garrincha and the new black prodigy, Pelé. And there was Zagalo, a player who covered vast tracts of ground at electric pace, one with lungs of leather and an astute footballing brain. The components were there, and the world waited to see whether they could be put together.

All four British teams competed; the Welsh and Irish for the first and – to date – last time. The former had a fine goalkeeper in Kelsey, the majestic John Charles, a clever inside-forward in Allchurch, an impish winger in Cliff Jones. The latter had Danny Blanchflower and Jimmy McIlroy, but the Munich air disaster had deprived them of Blanchflower's brother, Jackie, a commanding centre-back. Both teams thrived on the intimate atmosphere they created off the field, devoid of the paranoia and bitching that had surrounded English team selection.

To be fair to England, they had suffered terribly from Munich. The accident deprived them of Duncan Edwards, their brilliant left-half; Tommy Taylor, a dangerous centre-forward; and Roger Byrne, a resourceful back. Players such as these could not be replaced overnight, admittedly; but some of the

The last moments of the 1930 final in which Uruguay defeated Argentina 4–2. Here Hector Castro (just to left of right-hand upright) scores the Uruguayans' fourth goal. He was known as 'El Manco' (one-arm) after his right arm had been amputated at the elbow. *United Press International*

Left: The victorious Italian team that defeated Czechoslovakia in the 1934 final. From left, *standing*: Combi, Monti, Ferraris IV, Allemandi, Guita, Ferraris. *Kneeling*: Schiavio, Meazza, Monzeglio, Bertolini, Orsı. *Keystone Press Agency*

Above: World Cup 1938. A scene from the Italy–Brazil semi-final. The game for which the famous Brazilian forward, Leonidas, was 'rested'. Piola is the Italian in the dark shirt; Domingas, Machados and Walter the Brazilians (left to right). *Keystone Press Agency*

Right: The victorious Italian team after their 1938 final win over Hungary. Brandishing the Jules Rimet Trophy is Vittorio Pozzo, their mercurial manager, who had a great admiration for the British style of football. Just to *his* left is Piola, scorer of two goals against the Hungarians.

Keystone Press Agency

Below: Tejera and Gambetta (both Uruguay), Friaça (Brazil) and Maspoli (Uruguay) in a scene from the thrilling final game of the 1950 tournament, won 2–1 by Uruguay.

Associated Press

Above: A tight situation from the 1954 'Battle of Berne' between Brazil and Hungary. From left, Nilton Santos (Brazil), Castilho (Brazil), Toth (Hungary) and Brandaozinho (Brazil). Santos was later sent off for fighting, together with Boszik, the Hungarian captain.

Keystone Press Agency

From the 1954 final. Morlock, the German centre-forward, scores the first of his side's goals in their unexpected 3–2 victory over the Hungarian 'wunderteam'. *United Press International*.

Above: World Cup 1958. The gallant Welsh drew 0–0 in their qualifying group with Sweden, eventual finalists. Here the legendary John Charles forces Svensson to a save, with full-back Axbom in attendance.

Keystone Press Agency

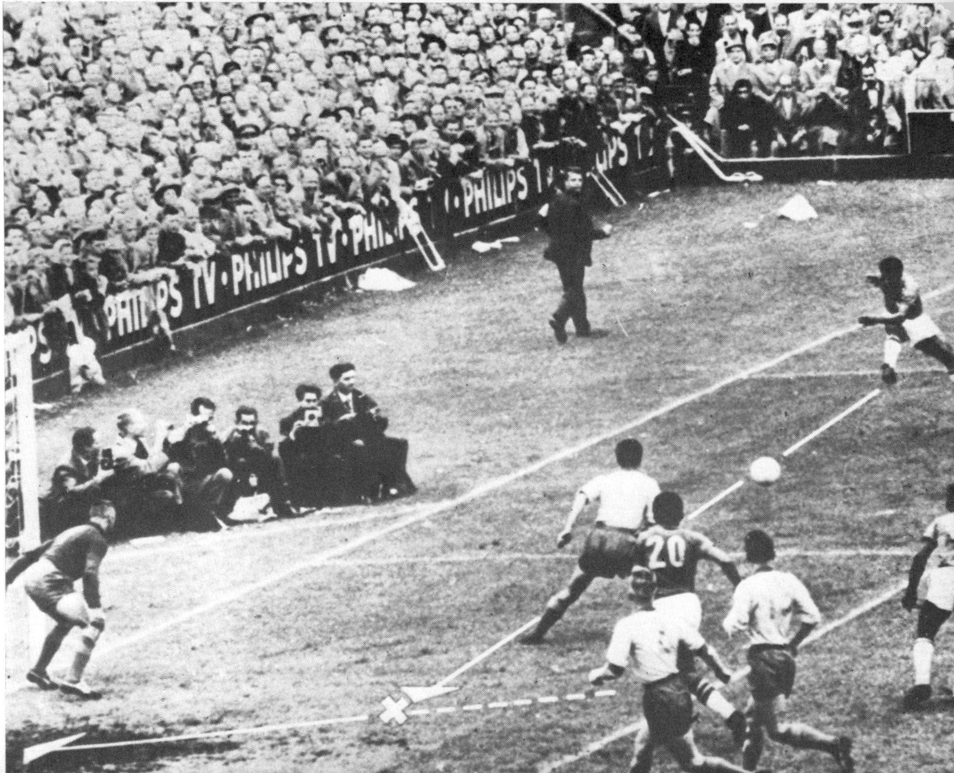

Right: From the 1958 final. The amazing Garrincha centres for Vavà (No. 20) to hammer in Brazil's first, and equalizing, goal.

United Press International

World Cup 1958. The victorious Brazilian team. From left to right, *standing*: trainer Djalma Santos, Zito, Bellini, Nilton Santos, Orlando, Gilmar. *Kneeling*: Garrincha, Didì, Pelé, Vavà, Zagalo, trainer. All but Bellini and Orlando would play four years later; and these two would be mysteriously recalled in 1966.
United Press International

World Cup 1962. Formidable winger against formidable full-back. Garrincha (Brazil) and Wilson (England) in a duel from the quarter-final tie in which the Brazilians won 3–1.

United Press International

Above: World Cup Final 1962. Djalma Santos (Brazil), Masopust (Czechoslovakia), Didì (Brazil) and Jelinek (Czechoslovakia) in an incident from the match that Brazil won 3–1. And where's the ball?
United Press International

Below: World Cup Final 1962. Mauro is unable to prevent Masopust from shooting home Czechoslovakia's only goal of the match past Gilmar, the Brazilian goalkeeper. Djalma Santos is the defender in the background.
Associated Press

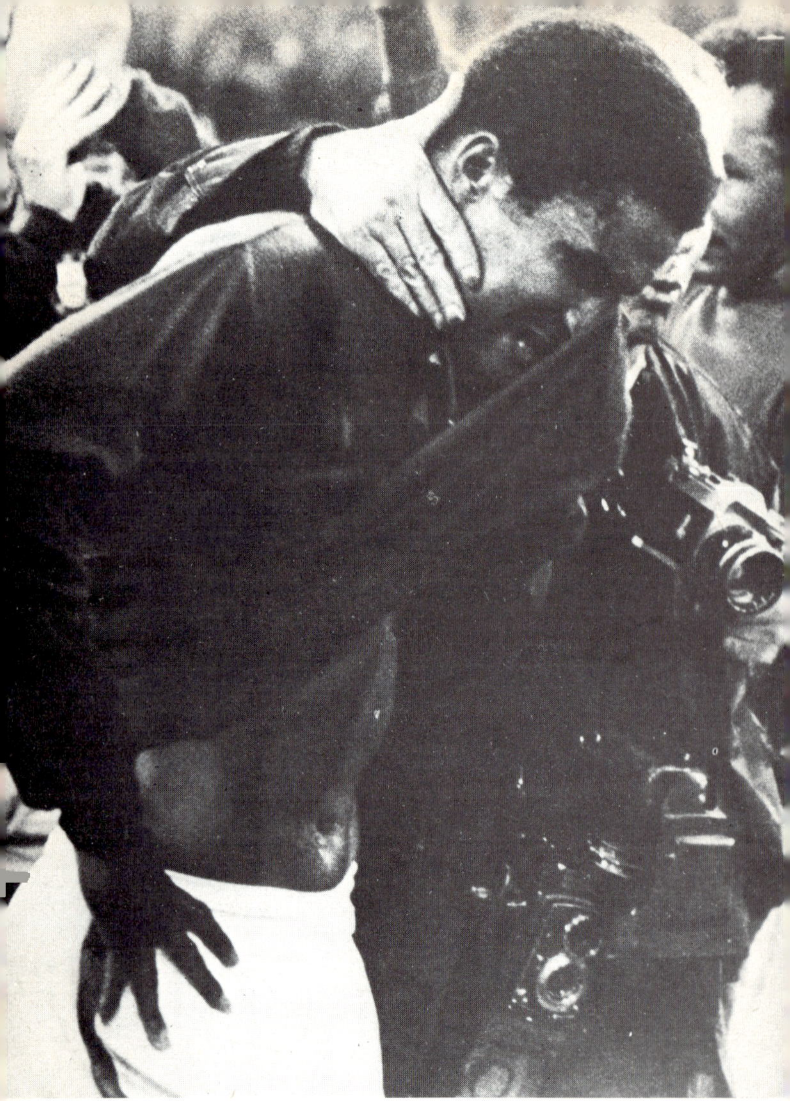

Above: World Cup 1966. The extraordinary Eusebio, in tears after Portugal's defeat by England in a thrilling semi-final tie. He would have the compensation of being the tournament's highest scorer. *BIPPA*

Right: World Cup Final 1966. Geoff Hurst scores England's final – and his third – goal in the 4–2 victory over West Germany. Wolfgang Overath is the German player nearby. *Syndication International*

ENGLAND 3 GERMANY W. 2

World Cup Final 1966. With seconds of normal time remaining, Weber slides the ball home for West Germany's equalizing goal. Other players shown, left to right, are Seeler, Cohen, Wilson, Moore, Schnellinger, Banks, Jack Charlton.

Keystone Press Agency

selection was bizarre in the extreme. Lofthouse was left at home, when his experience might have been invaluable; and Bobby Charlton, whose amazing swerve and lethal shooting had delighted everyone in the previous three months, was taken – only to be left on the touchlines for the whole tournament. Courage, it seemed, was lacking – the courage that often wins matches and tournaments.

The Scots had eliminated Spain but lost 4-0 to England in Glasgow. Few held out for them much hope of success. The Hungarians had lost too many of their star players in the aftermath of the 1956 Revolution, and such as remained were long in the tooth. Argentina competed, but without its much-famed 'Trio of Death' in the inside forward positions – Maschio, Angelillo and Sivori – all playing with Italian clubs and ignored. And the Germans seemed weak, despite the continued and cunning presence of Herberger, the coach.

The Russians competed for the first time, having won the 1956 Olympiad in Australia. They had the amazing Yachin in goal, kept themselves to themselves, and would play the sturdy sort of game that one has come to expect from them in recent years – functionalism with just the occasional flash of forward and midfield genius.

Playing at home, the Swedes called upon several of their stars based in Italy – the elegant Liedholm, tall and commanding in midfield; Nacka Skoglund, a hero of their 1950 World Cup team; Gustavsson, a commanding centre-back; and Kurt Hamrin, an electric little outside-right. To begin with, their supporters were pessimistic, but pessimism soon changed to optimism.

No one anticipated much from the French, yet they were to be the revelation of the tournament. In their first game, they walked through Paraguay 7-3, three of the goals coming from Juste Fontaine, who had come to the tournament not expecting to gain a place. He would score thirteen goals in all – a record that will not easily be beaten. And alongside Fontaine was Kopa – small, strong, beautifully-balanced with fine control and the ability to give a defence-splitting pass.

Group IV was the focal point – Brazil, Russia, England and Austria. The Brazilians beat the other two, drew a goalless game against England, who also drew with Russia and Austria. To a play-off, and the Russians came through by the one goal. If only Tom Finney had not been injured in the first game of the tournament. If only.

The Irish drew against the Germans, beat the Czechs, lost to Argentina – who finished bottom of the pool! They came through after a play-off against Czechoslovakia, by the odd goal in three, with McParland scoring his second goal of the game in the first period of extra time. Courage, in their case, had paid off.

The Scots drew with Yugoslavia, went down to both France and Paraguay. Better news from the Welsh, who went to a play-off in their pool against the Hungarians – and won 2–1 after trailing at half-time. The victory would put them through against Brazil, and few gave them much hope.

That especially after the 'real' Brazil had played for the first time in the third game of their qualifying group. Out had gone Jose Altafini, nicknamed 'Mazzola' for his resemblance to the great post-war Italian inside forward; a man who would play for Italy in the 1962 finals, who at the age of thirty-four would score against Derby County in the semi-final of the 1972–73 European Cup trophy goals that were *par excellence*, those of a venomous striker. And in would come Garrincha and Pelé.

Both were to have an extraordinary effect on the 1958 competition, an extraordinary effect on players and spectators throughout the world. Garrincha and Pelé – two of the great instinctive players of the age, of any age. The former was a winger who had all the powers of Matthews – the vicious swerve that took him outside the full back, the ability to accelerate into astonishing speed from a standing start. Despite – perhaps because of – a curiously twisted knee, a legacy from birth, his ball-control was exceptional. And Pelé, at seventeen, his head pointed like a coconut, with all his legendary skills already there for all to see – the ability to 'kill' a ball on thigh or chest, to shoot ferociously from impossible angles, to head a ball with a power that reminded people of Lawton or Kocsis.

So what chance Wales, against players such as these? In the event, much. If only John Charles had been fit to play, the one Welshman who could have put pressure on the Brazilian defence. As it was, the Welsh defence played superbly; and Pelé was later to describe the one goal of the match as the most important he had ever scored. And there's over a thousand to choose from!

Into the semi-finals with Brazil went France, Germany, Sweden. The Germans churned on, their ageing team and cunning management able to find answers to all the questions posed by the Yugoslavs. Sweden went through with Hamrin on venomous form – stockings rolled down, small and compact, hard to stop once he began to find his stride, scorer of the first goal against the Russians, maker of the second.

And there was France – the team no one was prepared to take seriously, even though they had won their qualifying group and scored eleven goals in the process. Against the Irish, Fontaine scored twice more to re-emphasise his effectiveness. Tired and depleted by injuries, the Irish had no cause for complaint. Their effort, like that of the Welsh, had been brave and dignified.

In the semi-finals, it was the turn of the French to suffer at the hands of Brazil. The score was still 1-1 when Jonquet, the elegant French centre-half was forced to retire in the thirty-seventh minute: a retirement that was to prove fatal as Pelé scored a hat trick and Brazil ran out winners 5-2. France would have consolation later, when they would defeat Germany in the match to decide third place by six goals to three, four coming from the incessant Fontaine.

Germany had proved no match for Sweden. The raucousness of German chanting at international matches is legendary, but in Sweden the German supporters found their match. As the Swedes progressed from round to round, so grew the noise of their fans, nationalist to the extreme. And so on the field, the Germans could find no answers to the wiles of Liedholm in midfield, the venom of Hamrin as he cut in from the wing. They would unearth a potentially great defender in Schnellinger, a powerful midfield player in Szymaniak – but the Germans knew that they deserved to be out.

In the Final, the Swedish crowd was silenced by FIFA. An official had attended the semi-final game, put a stop to organised cheering . . . and a Swedish crowd deprived of its cheerleaders would scarcely cheer at all. Just the once, as Liedholm put Sweden ahead after four minutes. 'When the Brazilians are a goal down,' had said George Raynor, Sweden's Yorkshire coach, 'they panic all over the show.' But Raynor must have been thinking of the overtrained 1954 Brazilians or the dazzling unpredictables of 1950.

Twice, it was Garrincha; twice he swerved maniacally past Swedish defenders and centred; twice Vavà rushed in to score. And ten minutes after half-time it was Pelé's turn. Trapping a long centre on his thigh, he hooked it over his head, slashed it into the net. He would score Brazil's fifth goal with his head after Zagalo had torn through for the fourth. And though Sweden would get a second goal, that would be that.

The crowd applauded as the Brazilians did two laps of honour, first with their own flag, then with that of the Swedes. Their supporters chanted '*samba, samba*'. And the world knew that it had seen a new style of football.

1958 – Final Stages

Quarter-Finals

FRANCE 4, IRELAND 0 (1-0) *Norrkoping*

FRANCE: Abbes; Kaelbel, Lerond; Penverne, Jonquet, Marcel; Wisnieski, Fontaine, Kopa, Piantoni, Vincent.
IRELAND: Gregg; Keith, McMichael; Blanchflower, Cunningham, Cush; Bingham, Casey, Scott, McIlroy, McParland.
SCORERS: Wisnieski, Fontaine (2), Piantoni for France.

GERMANY 1, YUGOSLAVIA 0 (1-0). *Malmo*

GERMANY: Herkenrath; Stollenwerk, Juskowiak; Eckel, Erhardt, Szymaniak; Rahn, Walter, Seeler, Schmidt, Schaefer.
YUGOSLAVIA: Krivocuka; Sijakovic, Crnkovic; Krstic, Zebec, Boskov; Petakovik, Veselinovic, Milutinovic, Ognjanovic, Rajkov.
SCORER: Rahn for Germany.

SWEDEN 2, RUSSIA 0 (0-0). *Stockholm*

SWEDEN: Svensson; Bergmark, Axbom; Boerjesson, Gustavsson, Parling; Hamrin, Gren, Simonsson, Liedholm, Skoglung.
RUSSIA: Yachin; Kessarev, Kuznetsov; Voinov, Krijevski, Tsarev; Ivanov, A., Ivanov, V., Simonian, Salnikov, Ilyin.
SCORERS: Hamrin, Simonsson for Sweden.

BRAZIL 1 WALES 0 (0-0). *Gothenburg*

BRAZIL: Gilmar; De Sordi, Santos, N.; Zito, Bellini, Orlando; Garrincha, Didì, Mazzola, Pelé, Zagalo.
WALES: Kelsey; Williams, Hopkins; Sullivan, Charles, M., Bowen; Medwin, Hewitt, Webster, Allchurch, Jones.
SCORER: Pelé for Brazil.

Semi-Finals

BRAZIL 5, FRANCE 2 (2-1). *Stockholm*

BRAZIL: Gilmar; De Sordi, Santos, N.; Zito, Bellini, Orlando; Garrincha, Didì, Vavà, Pelé, Zagalo.
FRANCE: Abbes; Kaelbel, Lerond; Penverne, Jonquet, Marcel; Wisnieski, Fontaine, Kopa, Piantoni, Vincent.
SCORERS: Vavà, Didì, Pelé (3) for Brazil; Fontaine, Piantoni for France.

SWEDEN 3, GERMANY 1 (1-1). *Gothenberg*

Sweden: Svensson; Bergmark, Axbom; Boerjesson, Gustavsson, Parling; Hamrin, Gren, Simonsson, Liedholm, Skoglund.
Germany: Herkenrath; Stollenwerk, Juskowiak; Eckel, Erhardt, Szymaniak; Rahn, Walter, Seeler, Schaefer, Cieslarczyk.
Scorers: Schaefer for Germany; Skoglund, Gren, Hamrin for Sweden.

Third Place Match

FRANCE 6, GERMANY 3 (0-0). *Gothenburg*

France: Abbes; Kaelberl, Lerond; Penverne, Lafont, Marcel; Wisnieski, Douis, Kopa, Fontaine, Vincent.
Germany: Kwiatowski; Stollenwerk, Erhardt; Schnellinger, Wewers, Szymaniak; Rahn, Sturm, Kelbassa, Schaefer, Cieslarczyk.
Scorers: Fontaine (4), Kopa, penalty, Douis for France; Cieslarczyk, Rahn, Schaefer for Germany.

Final

BRAZIL 5, SWEDEN 2 (2-1). *Stockholm*

Brazil: Gilmar; Santos, D., Santos, N.; Zito, Bellini, Orlando; Garrincha, Didì, Vavà, Pelé, Zagalo.
Sweden: Svensson; Bergmark, Axbom; Boerjesson, Gustavsson, Parling; Hamrin, Gren, Simonsson, Liedholm, Skoglund.
Scorers: Liedholm, Simonsson for Sweden; Vavà (2), Pelé (2), Zagalo for Brazil.

2 THE BRAZILIAN TRIUMPH CONTINUES – DESPITE A RUDE INTERRUPTION BY ENGLAND

World Cup 1962 – held in Chile

It should, perhaps, have been held in Argentina. But if Chile had recently had earthquakes, then the general antipathy towards Argentina in footballing circles had not lessened. And as a spokesman for the Chilean claim put it, they needed the World Cup '*because* we have nothing'. Cunning logic indeed; and the Chileans set about building a new stadium in Santiago to house a hysterical populace. (Cynics pointed out Chile had won nothing since the Pacific War in the middle of the nineteenth century.)

Brazil were the favourites, inevitably. They had two new centre-backs; and that was all. Garrincha, Zagalo, Didì and Pelé were still there – though the last would play only two games before being replaced by another exciting striker in Amarildo. And taken seriously with the Brazilians were the Russians – who on a recent South American tour had beaten Argentina, Uruguay and Chile.

England had played well on their way to Chile, beating Peru 4-0 in Lima. In Greaves and Charlton they had world class forwards; in Bobby Moore, a debutant in Lima, a defender of poise. But the self-confidence was not there, the forwards would fail time and again to find a way through the packed defences that would make a nonsense of the early part of the competition.

Italy arrived with Gianni Rivera in their ranks, arguably one of the really gifted players Europe has seen since the end of the war. Eighteen then, a precision passer of the ball and with a perfect sense of balance he would play one good game before being dropped. The Italians also brought with them a host of *Oriundi* – foreigners of Italian extraction – such as Altafini, Sormani, Maschio and Sivori. A strong team on paper, but football matches are not won on paper – and the Italian campaign would be catastrophic.

After a goalless draw against Germany, the Italians found themselves involved in yet another of those World Cup 'battles' when they came to play Chile in Santiago. At the root of the trouble were some silly newspaper articles written by Italian journalists, critical of the organisation of the tournament, critical of the squalor of Santiago, critical of the morals of Chilean womanhood. From the start of the game the Chileans spat at the Italians, fouled them viciously. Ironic, therefore, that the two players sent off in the game should both have been Italian; while a left hook thrown by Sanchez, the Chilean winger – one that broke Maschio's nose – went unseen by the referee. Two-nil to Chile, and the Italians were effectively out of the tournament.

Germany won that second group, with Schnellinger powerful in defence, Seeler powerful in attack, Szymaniak destroying everything in midfield. They had come up with a useful inside-forward in Helmut Haller, who would find fame in Italy in later years and compete in two further World Cups. And the Chileans, inevitably, came through.

In group III, Brazil beat Mexico 2-0; were held to a goalless draw by the unfancied Czechs – a game in which Pelé pulled a muscle, and was lost to the rest of the tournament; then beat Spain, with Amarildo – Pelé's replacement – getting both goals in a 2-1 victory. The Czechs went through even though they had lost one of their games, drawn another.

In group I, the Russians won a violent yet exciting game against Yugoslavia 2-0; then were involved in an extraordinary match against the Columbians, who after being 3-0 down in the first fifteen minutes took the final score to 4-4. Yachin in goal had a sad game, sad enough for some commentators to prophesy the end of the greatest goalkeeper of modern times. Premature indeed, if only for Yachin's fine displays in England four years later. Yugoslavia would go through to the quarter-finals with Russia, their little inside-forward, Sekularac, one of the men of the tournament.

And so to group IV, where the Hungarians looked a fine side. In Florian Albert they had unearthed a centre-forward of high gifts, another who would do marvellously in 1966. And in Solymosi, the right-half, they had a player of relaxed quality. These two were highly responsible for the 2-1 defeat of the English side in the first game; the 6-1 thrashing administered to Bulgaria in the second.

As for England, they played good football – with Bobby Charlton on great form – to defeat the Argentinians 3-1. Alan Peacock made his debut, and a fine one. But in the final game against the Bulgarians, the English could find no way through a massed defence, had to be content with a goalless draw. They were through, but few would dare to class them with the Hungarians.

In the event, they met – and were beaten by – Brazil. The 3-1 scoreline seemed slightly unjust; but Garrincha was in devastating form, seemingly having added to his vast repertoire of tricks the ability to head a ball viciously. And though Hitchens equalised for England before half-time, two mistakes by Springett in goal gave goals to Vavà and Amarildo after the interval.

No surprise, that result, but surprises elsewhere. Chile, for example, came through against Russia – with Yachin still inexplicably tense in goal, and the crowd manic in its joy. Not for the first or last time, the 'home' team had confounded early prognostication.

And Hungary went out. For eighty of the ninety minutes against the Czechs Hungary attacked, inflicting serious damage on the Czech crossbar and posts. Nothing, it seemed, would ever be a few millimetres farther in the right direction; and though Solymosi and Albert did everything that was asked of them, their team ever trailed to an early, thirteenth-minute goal from the Czech inside-forward, Scherer.

In the last quarter-final tie, the Yugoslavs put out the Germans. Only four minutes of the game remained when Galic, the inside-left, dribbled his way through the German defence and passed to Radakovic – head bandaged after a collision – to score. But the Germans could have had little reason for complaint. In Sekularac, the Yugoslavs had one of the best midfield players of the tournament; in Soskic a strong, agile goalkeeper; in Markovic, a commanding centre-back, who on the day would outplay the formidable Uwe Seeler.

In the semi-finals, it was the turn of Chile to fall before the devastating Garrincha. He scored the first of four Brazilian goals with a fierce left-foot shot, the second with another of his new-found trampoline-like headers. And though the Chileans hit back with a goal before half-time from Toro, two further goals – this time from Vavà – in the second half, and only a penalty in return, put the Brazilians through.

Not, however, without tremblings. In the second half of the game Garrincha himself was expelled for kicking retaliatorily at a Chilean opponent; and then suffered the indignity of having his head cut open by a bottle thrown from the crowd as he was leaving the pitch. In the event, the injury was not serious, the threat of suspension from the Final very real. It was said, however, that the President of Brazil had listened to the game on headphones during Mass; that he had appealed personally to the disciplinary committee on Garrincha's behalf. The brilliant winger would play in the Final after receiving a caution.

The opposition to Brazil would be provided by the Czechs, victors in the other semi-final against Yugoslavia. As in the quarter-final, the Czechs had much less of the play; but this time took their chances well, scoring three goals, conceding one. Masopust controlled the midfield; the other two half-backs, Pluskal and Popluhar, sealed up the middle of the defence with rugged authority; Kvasniak ambled round in the forward line prompting and guiding. And the weary Yugoslavs were left to lose the match for third place, by the one goal and against a Chilean side again whipped on by a partisan crowd.

As in 1958, Brazil gave away the first goal of the Final –

Masopust scoring in the fourteenth minute after having run on to an exquisite through pass from Scherer; as in 1958, the team's reaction was swift and interesting. It was Pelé's replacement, Amarildo, who scored, running almost to the left-hand goal line with the ball, screwing an extraordinary shot past Schroiff, the Czech goalkeeper, who had positioned himself perfectly at the near post to narrow the angle.

One-one, then, at half-time; and when Brazil scored again in the sixty-ninth minute, good goal though it was, it came against the run of the play. Amarildo it was who collected a pass from Zito, cut past a defender and crossed for Zito himself to charge in and head just under the bar. Thus was the slightly one-paced elegance of Masopust and Kvasniak rewarded; and salt was further rubbed into the wound twelve minutes from time when Djalma Santos hooked a centre high into the Czech penalty area, Schroiff lost its flight against the glare of the sun, lost it when it hit the ground, and Vavà snapped in to score, 3-1, seemingly a convincing win; but Garrincha had been well controlled, Didì had been obscure.

Brazil had won the Cup for the second time, but with little of the flair that they had shown in Sweden. True, Pelé had been absent for the important games, and Pelé might have made a considerable difference. The Brazilians, however, had been forced to use Zagalo as a deep-lying winger, and the 4-2-4 formation of 1958 had wilted into the 4-3-3 of 1962, would even tempt people to think of four midfield players and only two genuine strikers.

More serious, it had been a disappointing tournament. The great Puskas, taking time off from scoring goals for his new club, Real Madrid, said of the football he had seen that it was 'war'. The qualifying games had provided a string of disappointments, defensive skill had been at a premium. The tournament in Sweden had provided 119 goals, that in Chile thirty less; and where Fontaine had scored so freely in 1958, the highest figure that any individual goalscorer would reach in Chile was four.

1962 – Final Stages

Quarter-Finals

YUGOSLAVIA 1, GERMANY 0 (0-0). *Santiago*

YUGOSLAVIA: Soskic; Durkovic, Jusufi; Radakovic, Markovic, Popovic; Kovacevic, Sekularac, Jerkovic, Galic, Skoblar.
GERMANY: Fahrian; Novak, Schnellinger; Schultz, Erhardt, Giesemann; Haller, Szymaniak, Seeler, Brulls, Schaefer.
SCORER: Radakovic for Yugoslavia.

BRAZIL 3, ENGLAND 1 (1-1). *Viña del Mar*

BRAZIL: Gilmar; Santos D., Mauro, Zozimo, Santos, N.; Zito, Didì; Garrincha, Vavà, Amarildo, Zagalo.
ENGLAND: Springett; Armfield, Wilson; Moore, Norman, Flowers; Douglas, Greaves, Hitchens, Haynes, Charlton.
SCORERS: Garrincha (2), Vavà for Brazil; Hitchens for England.

CHILE 2, RUSSIA 1 (2-1). *Arica*

CHILE: Escutti; Eyzaguirre, Contreras, Sanchez, R., Navarro; Toro, Rojas; Ramirez, Landa, Tobar, Sanchez, L.
RUSSIA: Yachin; Tchokelli, Ostrovski; Voronin, Maslenkin, Netto; Chislenko, Ivanov, Ponedelnik, Mamikin, Meshki.
SCORERS: Sanchez, L., Rojas for Chile; Chislenko for Russia.

CZECHOSLOVAKIA 1, HUNGARY 0 (1-0). *Rancagua*

CZECHOSLOVAKIA: Schroiff; Lala, Novak; Pluskal, Popluhar, Masopust; Pospichal, Scherer, Kvasniak, Kadraba, Jelinek.
HUNGARY: Grosics; Matrai, Sarosi; Solymosi, Meszoly, Sipos; Sandor, Rakosi, Albert, Tichy, Fenyvesi.
SCORER: Scherer for Czechoslovakia.

Semi-Finals

BRAZIL 4, CHILE 2 (2-1). *Santiago*

BRAZIL: Gilmar; Santos, D., Mauro, Zozimo, Santos, N.; Zito, Didì; Garrincha, Vavà, Amarildo, Zagalo.
CHILE: Escutti; Eyzaguirre, Contreras, Sanchez, R., Rodriguez; Toro, Rojas; Ramirez, Landa, Tobar, Sanchez, L.
SCORERS: Garrincha (2), Vavà (2), for Brazil; Toro, Sanchez, L. (penalty) for Chile.

CZECHOSLOVAKIA 3, YUGOSLAVIA 1 (0-0). *Vina del Mar*

CZECHOSLOVAKIA: Schroiff; Lala, Novak; Pluskal, Popluhar, Masopust; Pospichal, Scherer, Kvasniak, Kadraba, Jelinek.
YUGOSLAVIA: Soskic; Durkovic, Jusufi; Radakovic, Markovic, Popovic; Sujakovic, Sekularac, Jerkovic, Galic, Skoblar.
SCORERS: Kadraba, Scherer (2), for Czechoslovakia; Jerkovic for Yugoslavia.

Third Place Match

CHILE: Godoy; Eyzaguirre, Cruz, Sanchez, R., Rodriguez; Toro, Rojas; Ramirez, Campos, Tobar, Sanchez, L.
YUGOSLAVIA: Soskic; Durkovic, Svinjarevic; Radakovic, Markovic, Popovic; Kovacevic, Sekularac, Jerkovic, Galic, Skoblar.
SCORER: Rojas for Chile.

Final

BRAZIL 3, CZECHOSLOVAKIA 1 (1-1). *Santiago*

BRAZIL: Gilmar; Santos, D., Mauro, Zozimo, Santos, N.; Zito, Didì; Garrincha, Vavà, Amarildo, Zagalo.
CZECHOSLOVAKIA: Schroiff; Tichy, Novak; Pluskal, Popluhar, Masopust; Pospichal, Scherer, Kvasniak, Kadraba, Jelinek.
SCORERS: Masopust for Czechoslovakia; Amarildo, Zito, Vavà for Brazil.

World Cup 1966 – held in England

When he took over from Walter Winterbottom the managership of the English national side, Alf Ramsey promised that England would win the 1966 tournament. They did and he did; for there had been fewer stronger examples in the history of the game of 'the players' manager'. It was Nobby Stiles who said it after England had beaten Germany in the Final. '*You* did it, Alf,' he cried tearfully. 'We'd have been nothing without you.'

England had to be favourites, given home advantage, given a successful Scandinavian tour just before the series began. On paper they had a fine goalkeeper in Banks, a potential match-winner in Greaves, a gifted and well-drilled defence. But in midfield they relied on Bobby Charlton, always known as a striker. In the event Charlton would play superbly in the semi-final; bc decisive in the Final. But those days were ahead.

Eyes also turned inevitably towards Brazil during their Scandinavian tour. But it was clear that the great days were passed. If Pelé was still there, threatening as ever, there were many questions that received unsatisfactory answers. Who would fill in for Zagalo, with his tireless and effective running? Who was there to replace the immaculate Didì? Was Garrincha sufficiently recovered from a car crash and a series of serious knee operations? In fact, so strange an amalgam was the Brazilian party between unproven young players and older hands that they brought with them the very two defenders they had omitted on grounds of old age four years earlier – Bellini and Orlando.

Russia still had Yachin, still lacked the spark that makes triumphant teams. The Italians had three stylish inside-forwards in Mazzola, Rivera and Bulgarelli, an accomplished goal-scoring back in the giant Facchetti. They had beaten Argentina 3-0 just before the competition opened. But they also had a reputation for playing below form away from home. And the Argentinians that day had fielded something of a reserve side.

The Germans still had the indomitable Seeler up front, the indestructible Schnellinger in defence. It was known that they lacked a good goalkeeper, but had unearthed a fine young attacking wing-half in Beckenbauer, still had Helmut Haller to give guidance in midfield, and in Wolfgang Overath possessed another midfield player of the highest skill and fierce ability to read the patterns of a game.

The Brazilians were undoubtedly drawn in the toughest group – against Bulgaria, Hungary and Portugal. They won the opening game, against the first of these three, lost the other two. Against the Bulgarians both goals came from freekicks, a cannonball from Pelé, a 'banana' shot from Garrincha; and Pelé spent much of the match trying to avoid scything tackles.

The Brazilians then came across Hungary, losers to Portugal in their first game thanks to some desperately inefficient goalkeeping. (More than one authority thought that Hungary would have won this competition had they been served in goal even remotely well.) The Hungarians had Albert, one of their heroes four years previously; they had a fine new forward in Bene, who had played superbly in the winning 1964 Olympic team; they had another hero from 1962 in Meszoly, always prepared to break into attack from behind; and they had Farkas, a deadly finisher close to goal.

Without Pelé, the Brazilians looked feeble indeed. Garrincha looked creaky, the two elder statesmen of the defence – Djalma Santos and Bellini – ominously static. Against fast and tricky running, that Brazilian defence crumbled quickly. Bene swerved and knifed through the middle after three minutes of play to slide the ball home; and although Brazil equalised through the young Tostao just before half-time, their goal came against all justice.

It was in the second half that their fate was sealed. First Albert ran through, slid the ball to Bene on the right, and Farkas rushed in to smack home the volleyed cross – as spectacular a goal as the competition was to see. And then came a penalty, tucked home by Meszoly. The Liverpool crowd rose to the Hungarians, and particularly Albert; the Brazilians went back to camp to plan survival against Portugal.

They did for this match what they might have done earlier –

play young men capable of running for ninety minutes. Pelé came back clearly not fit, and was put out of the game early on by a vicious tackle from Morais, one that failed to receive from the too placid English referee the punishment it deserved – expulsion. All those who saw it will never forget the sight of Pelé, his face agonised, lying by the touchline swathed in a blanket.

The game against Hungary had been Brazil's first defeat in a World Cup match since 1954 – when they had been put out in that infamous game – by the Hungarians. The Portugal game showed that they deserved to be out. They had no answers to Albert, Bene and Farkas; now they had no answers to the fast running and powerful shooting of Eusebio. It was the famous coloured player from Mozambique who smashed in a shot in the fourteenth minute – for Manga, the Brazilian goalkeeper to shovel it away into the path of Simoes. A headed goal from Eusebio, then a right-foot shot – and Brazil (despite Rildo's second-half score) were out. They caught the train to Euston complaining – rightly – of inefficient refereeing. But they had proved the point that great teams are made up of great players, that greatness is not bestowed magically from above to those countries who feel they deserve it.

Elsewhere Argentina and West Germany came through from group II, the former gathering a reputation for ruthlessness that would serve to dim appreciation of their undoubted skills. Both teams beat Switzerland and Spain, their game together was drawn. The West Germans looked classy in a 5-0 victory over Switzerland. They still had their own goalkeeping problems; but the defence remained firm, the midfield enterprising. As for Spain, they used their older players initially – and like Brazil came to rue their choice. When they did put out their youngsters, it was against the Germans and too late, despite a spirited performance.

England came through in the first group, desperately unconvincing. Against Uruguay they were unable to pierce the defensive barrier; against Mexico it took a superb, spectacular shot from long-distance and Bobby Charlton to break the deadlock; against

France they looked unconvincing against a team down to ten men for much of the game. The English defence, however, appeared impressive; fortunately indeed to have a goalkeeper of Banks' class in a year of so much bad goalkeeping. The Uruguayans beat France, drew with Mexico, to join them.

Up in the North-east it was nearly all Russia. They disposed of North Korea in the opening game, scoring three goals in the process; then scored just the one goal against a lethargic Italian team bereft of Rivera's skills. As so often Italian caution in team selection and tactics brought its just rewards. But they still had to play North Korea – a game that should have given them little cause for sleeplessness.

In the event, the game was as big a shock as England's defeat at the hands of the Americans sixteen years earlier. Though the Italians lost Bulgarelli in the thirty-fourth minute with strained ligaments (an injury caused by his own foul tackle), they throughout played like ghosts. Pak Doo Ik it was who scored the only goal of the match just before half-time, and when the final whistle came, the Middlesbrough crowd rushed on to the pitch in joy. Who could ever forget the sight of one enormous British sailor tucking a Korean player under each arm and rushing round the pitch like a lunatic. As for the Italians they went home in shame, were pelted with rotten vegetables on arrival at Genoa airport at the dead of night.

Two of the quarter-finals remain memorable – and for totally differing reasons. The Russians won by the odd goal in three against the Hungarians, manifestly less imaginative, but having in goal a Yachin instead of a Gelei; and at Sheffield the West Germans won 4–0 against a dispirited and disorganised Uruguayan team that had two men sent off and never really tried to stay in the game.

London and Liverpool would see the more fascinating matches. For their game against Argentina at Wembley, England left out the injured Jimmy Greaves (and were perhaps glad to do so, for his form had been disappointing) and brought in Geoff Hurst – whose last game, against Denmark, had been disastrously uninspiring. As so often happens in these things,

Hurst turned out to be the match-winner, scoring the only goal of the game thirteen minutes from time; and once forcing Roma, the Argentinian goalkeeper, to an acrobatic windmill-like save at point-blank range.

Everything, however, came to be overshadowed in most people's minds by the events just before half-time when Rattin, the South Americans' captain, was sent off by the German referee, Herr Kreitlin, for objecting to the booking of one of his team mates. Rattin himself had been booked for a trip on Bobby Charlton; but though there had been many nasty and cynical Argentinian fouls, that particular one had been by no means the worst. Later the referee claimed to have sent off Rattin 'for the look on his face'. In the event the game was held up for eleven minutes while Rattin refused to move, while the Argentinian coach, Juan Carlos Lorenzo argued from the touchline, while officials tried to get the game restarted. So the Argentinians lost the most effective player in midfield; and there can be little doubt that had they initially gone out to play as well as they could, the result might have been very different. Certainly England's eleven players made heavy work of the game in the second half against ten opponents bent merely on destructive tactics.

After the game officials moved quickly to protect the referee against the Argentinian reserves, who joined their colleagues to pound on the door of the English dressing-room, to make insinuating gestures and statements to World Cup officials. One of their players urinated on the floor outside the English quarters, their manager rubbed forefinger and thumb meaningfully together, and Alf Ramsey was distressed enough to refer to them as 'animals' in a remark that he later – understandably grudgingly – was forced to withdraw.

England were through, the mundanity of their play masked by events off the ball. And in the semi-finals they would meet Portugal, winners against the North Koreans in a game as extraordinary as that at Wembley. After their bizarre and heart-warming achievements against the Italians, the Koreans took on Eusebio and his men, nipping about smartly. A goal in the first minute was a fine tonic; two more soon after and the fancied Portuguese were three down.

That was the point at which Eusebio must have realised that Nemesis was staring him in the face. He ran through for one goal, smashed home a penalty after Torres had had his legs taken from underneath him, added two further goals in the second half. Augusto got a fifth, from a corner, and the Koreans were finally forced out, having given vast entertainment, having puzzled everyone as to the nature of their achievement. Everyone knew that for months they had lived in solitary and rigorous confinement. But the quickness with which they had learnt made many people wonder whether future competitions wouldn't deserve greater participation on the part of teams drawn from those countries with little footballing tradition.

Given the magnificent way in which Lancashire – and particularly Liverpool – had supported its games in the competition, Liverpudlians deserved much better than they received from the Russia–Germany semi-final, little more nor less than a war of attrition. Sabo made a potentially vicious tackle on Beckenbauer – only to come away limping himself; a long-range sliding effort from Schnellinger on Chislenko left that Russian limping. He went off for treatment, returned, lost a ball to Held, chased the German and was rightly sent off by Concetto Lo Bello, the famous Italian referee. Haller it was who scored the first German goal a minute before half time, just after Schnellinger's tackle; and Beckenbauer curled a shot around the Russian defensive wall for the second. Porkujan replied for Russia, but too late. And although the Russian manager publicly blamed Yachin for the two German goals, the truth was that without him they might have ceded two or three in the first twenty minutes.

The England–Portugal semi-final provided a pleasant and enthralling contrast. It was in this game that the English really came together to look formidable, the defence strong as ever, Bobby Charlton stupendous in midfield and behind the attack in a performance that must have gone a long way to earning him the award as European Footballer of the Year. Everything he tried, and he tried everything, came off. His swerving runs, long passing, ferocious shooting – all were in evidence. He it was who scored the first goal, after José Pereira had pushed out a shot from Hunt; and just as important, every Portuguese player he passed on the way back to the centre circle stopped to shake his hand.

From first whistle to last the game was played at an electrifying pace, graced by electric skills. There was the battle between Torres and Jack Charlton, two giants in the air; that between Stiles and Eusebio, with the heart and guts of the former matched against the amazing skills of the latter; and there was the battle in midfield between Charlton and the Portuguese captain, Coluna, with his casual talent for passing, his instinctual reading of the game. When Hurst raced through eleven minutes from the end and cut the ball back from the by line for Charlton to hammer in his second goal, that seemed that. But three minutes later Jack Charlton was forced to give away a penalty, taken and scored by Eusebio. And the last few minutes were played out in a frenzy – Stiles making a fine last-ditch tackle on Simoes, Banks going down brilliantly to a vicious shot from Coluna. England were through to the Final; and though Eusebio left the pitch in tears, comforted by his team mates, he would have the consolation (admittedly small) of scoring in Portugal's victory over Russia for the third place match, and thus consolidate his position as the tournament's leading scorer.

The Final would prove as dramatic as the changes in the weather – now brilliant sunshine, now driving rain; certainly the most dramatic Final that the competition has ever seen. It was the Germans who took the lead – in the thirteenth minute after Ray Wilson – normally so cool at fullback – had nonchalantly headed a loose ball down to the feet of Haller, for the German inside-forward to slide the ball past Banks. It was a lead Germany would hold for only six minutes – until Hurst turned in a free-kick taken too swiftly by Bobby Moore.

It was eighteen minutes into the second-half before England took the lead. For much of the match Alan Ball had run Schnellinger ragged – Schnellinger, thought of by many as the best fullback in the world. Time after time Ball had forced him away

RUSSIA 2, HUNGARY 1 (1-0) *Sunderland*

RUSSIA: Yachin; Ponomarev, Chesternjiev, Voronin, Danilov; Sabo, Khusainov; Chislenko, Banichevski, Malafeev, Porkujan.
HUNGARY: Gelei; Matrai; Kaposzta, Meszoly, Sipos, Szepesi; Nagy, Albert, Rakosi; Bene, Farkas.
SCORERS: Chislenko, Porkujan for Russia; Bene for Hungary.

Semi-Finals

WEST GERMANY 2, RUSSIA 1(1-0). *Everton*

WEST GERMANY: Tilkowski; Hottges, Weber, Schultz, Schnellinger; Beckenbauer, Haller, Overath, Seeler, Held, Emmerich.
RUSSIA: Yachin; Ponomarev, Chesternjiev, Voronin, Danilov; Sabo, Khusainov; Chislenko, Banichevski, Malafeev, Porkujan.
SCORERS: Haller, Beckenbauer for Germany; Porkujan for Russia.

ENGLAND 2, PORTUGAL 1 (1-0). *Wembley*

ENGLAND: Banks (Leicester City); Cohen (Fulham), Wilson (Everton); Stiles (Manchester United), Charlton, J. (Leeds United), Moore (West Ham United); Ball (Blackpool), Hurst (West Ham United), Charlton, R. (Manchester United), Hunt (Liverpool), Peters (West Ham United).
PORTUGAL: José Pereira; Festa, Baptista, Carlos, Hilario; Graça, Coluna, Augusto; Eusebio, Torres, Simoes.
SCORERS: Charlton, R. (2) for England; Eusebio (penalty) for Portugal.

Third Place Match

PORTUGAL 2, RUSSIA 1 (1-1). *Wembley*
PORTUGAL: José Pereira; Festa, Baptista, Carlos, Hilario; Graça, Coluna, Augusto; Eusebio, Torres, Simoes.
RUSSIA: Yachin; Ponomarev, Khurtsilava, Korneev, Danilov; Voronin, Sichinava; Metreveli, Malafeev, Banichevski, Serebrianikov.
SCORERS: Eusebio (penalty), Torres for Portugal; Malafeev for Russia.

Final

ENGLAND 4, WEST GERMANY 2 (1-1) (2-2) after extra time. *Wembley*
ENGLAND: Banks; Cohen, Wilson; Stiles, Charlton, J., Moore; Ball, Hurst, Charlton, R., Hunt, Peters.
WEST GERMANY: Tilkowski; Hottges, Schultz; Weber, Schnellinger, Haller; Beckenbauer, Overath, Seeler, Held, Emmerich.
SCORERS: Hurst (3), Peters for England; Haller, Weber for Germany.

World Cup 1970 – held in Mexico

Given that the tournament tended to be played alternately in Europe and South America, it was inevitable that Mexico would be a venue sooner or later. For many, however, the 'later' would have been preferable. The 1968 Olympiad had shown precisely and agonisingly the problems thrown up in expecting top-class athletes to compete at high altitudes. And few parts of central Mexico were at less than 6–7,000 feet above sea level. The nonchalant could at least pretend that it made life more interesting.

What could have been prevented – and wasn't – was the callous selling-out of the tournament to financial interests. Too many games were played in noonday heat – merely to satisfy European television companies eager to televise games at peak viewing times. England, for example, played their vital group match against Brazil at noon, in temperatures of nearly 100 degrees and there was barely an England player who had not lost eight or ten pounds in weight as a result of dehydration.

England's preparations had been thorough enough. The team arrived in Mexico well before the tournament started; good accommodation had been found; supplies of food and drink had been flown out (though the Mexican customs officials appeared un-cooperative at first); the players were even supplied with reading material by Coronet Books, one of the country's leading paperback publishing firms. Leaving Mexico for a short tour, England won handsome victories over Columbia and Ecuador, the defence seemingly as ungenerous as it had been in 1966.

It was after the second of these games, as the team stopped off in Bogota on the way back to Mexico that Bobby Moore, the English captain, was absurdly accused of having stolen a bracelet from a hotel jewellers. Much has been written about this extraordinary incident, that would last for nearly two years, until the 'charges' were finally dropped. The important point to underline is Moore's amazing coolness during the whole affair. In a situation where many players might have cracked under the nervous strain imposed by being unable to fly back to Mexico with the rest of the team, of having to remain in a state of semi-solitary confinement while the matter was tentatively cleared up Moore was simply magnificent. Within days he was to go out and prove to the world that, as in 1966, he remained the best defensive wing-half in modern football.

If England had Moore, then Brazil still had Pelé. The Brazilians had taken, only months before the Finals, the extraordinary step of sacking their manager, the bubbling Joao Saldanha, and replacing him with Mario Zagalo, one of the heroes of 1958 and 1962. No one doubted the Brazilian talent. If they had a goalkeeper of laughable mediocrity in Felix, if their defence seemed unsound – then they had Gerson in midfield and up front Jairzinho and Tostao. The latter had recently undergone eye surgery, but was known to be a formidable foil to Pelé. The first few games would tell all about Brazil.

The West Germans were there also, eager for the chance to revenge their defeat at the hands of the English four years previously. The bulk of that side remained, they had two incisive wingers in Grabowski and Libuda, a 'new' goalkeeper in Maier, one of the best of the tournament. And that is not meant disparagingly. One of the many contrasts between the 1966 competition and that to be held in Mexico would be the overall improvement in goalkeeping standards. Banks (England), Kavazashvili (Russia), Piot (Belgium), Calderon (Mexico), Albertosi (Italy) and Mazurkiewicz (Uruguay) – all, with Maier, kept goal well in conditions that were far from helpful, ones in which the ball moved fast through the rarefied air, swerving and dipping unexpectedly, ones in which the brightness of the light put a premium on good judgement. We might note here that the fearsome Gerd Muller, who would score most goals in the tournament, came to face only two of the above-mentioned, when Germany played their semi-final against Italy and their final game against Uruguay.

The Italians came strangely, having qualified with some ease against East Germany and Wales in their preliminary group. In Riva they had a striker of renown, his left foot a terrifying weapon when given the chance to exercise itself. But too often Riva's brilliant goals had camouflaged weaknesses in the defence, lack of understanding in midfield. Mazzola was there for the second time, Rivera for the third – both players of high technical accomplishment, and supposedly unable to play together. The Italians decided in favour of the *staffeta*, a system whereby Mazzola would play the first half of each game, Rivera the second. The latter found it unacceptable, said so loudly, was nearly sent home as punishment, stayed, and in two games at least, would prove that he is one of the world's great intuitive players.

The Russians looked solid as ever, with Kavazashvili a worthy successor in goal to the great Yachin, and Shesternev a sweeper little behind Bobby Moore in terms of technical expertise and tactical acumen. They had an interesting young striker in Bishovets, but would play a type of football that lacked genuine inventiveness. Uruguay were another team strong on paper, again served brilliantly in goal (by Mazurkiewicz, one of the very small clutch of good goalkeepers four years previously), and with some terrifyingly robust defenders. One remembers particularly Montero Castillo in the centre of the field, Ubinas and Ancheta elsewhere. And the joker in the pack had to be Peru, coached for the tournament by Didì, the Brazilian ex-player and perennial hero of 1954, 1958 and 1962. It was known that they had some forwards of dazzling technical gifts, but did they have a team, could they put together a game?

Generally speaking those teams that were expected to come through, came through. The first game of the first group – and the tournament – was that between Mexico (the hosts) and Russia. A goalless draw, as with its 1966 counterpart, sounded an ominous warning. But Belgium played some light, waltzing football to beat El Salvador the following day; and when they came to meet Russia, deserved better than the 4-1 defeat that they allowed to be inflicted upon them. Bishovets scored two of those goals, Shesternev marshalled the defence superbly; and it was one of those days when the Russians showed the world just what they could do when prepared to cast off thoughts of weighty preparation and over-drilled tactics. And in the final game of the group, the Mexicans went through against the Belgians 1-0, thanks to a hotly disputed penalty decision, one that seemed to have been not uninfluenced by the frenzy of a vast home crowd. Mexico, unconvincingly, and Russia through, then, from that group.

Group II looked good for both Italy and Uruguay. Israel looked too raw, Sweden – despite the presence of one or two players of high talent, such as Kindvall and Grahn, who played their club football outside Sweden – lacked strength in depth. They it was who first faced Italy, going down to a drive from some long range delivered by the Italian midfield player, Domenghini, who throughout the tournament would play with a ubiquity that perilously ignored the heat of the sun and the rarity of the air. The Uruguayans scraped through 2-0 against Israel, more importantly lost Pedro Rocha, their midfield general after only a few minutes of play. It was an injury that would force the South

American team even further back on to their defensive and uncompromising heels, for Rocha would take no further part in the tournament.

The next match brought these two teams together into a goalless draw, with both sets of players full of hostility (both masked and overt). Riva was to claim that from the first Uruguayan defenders had spat at him whenever they were close; which did not excuse his lethargy. More dreary football was to follow, and the results continued to prove evidence of the essentially defensive attitudes that permeated group matches. The Swedes beat the Uruguayans, who went through on a marginally better goal average; and the Italians got through with two goalless draws and that one win. Top of the group with only one goal in three matches: that, surely, couldn't be the stuff of which world champions were made?

Group III was, indubitably, the toughest on paper; and certainly the matches from that group provided some of the most fascinating football. If the English won their first game against Rumania, they did so with some lack of ease, thanks to a goal from Geoff Hurst in the seventieth minute, and despite some sadistic tackling by the Rumanian defenders, a certain Mocanu in particular. If the Brazilians appeared to thrash the Czechs 4-1, it must be remembered that Petras scored the first goal of the match for Czechoslovakia, that they were served with some indifferent goalkeeping, that the third Brazilian goal (scored by Jairzinho) looked suspiciously offside. But Pelé was on superb form, scored an extraordinary goal; Rivelino put another in from a swerving free-kick; Jairzinho scored again, always threatened when he had possession; and Gerson in midfield sprayed accurate passes around with high panache, underlining the thought that so many of the world's finest distributors have been players whose athleticism was far from robust. Gerson, for example, is something of a one-paced player (and that pace never faster than slow-medium) who is a compulsive cigarette smoker. Hardly the stuff of which the textbook heroes are made, but a player of great influence.

Too many people – and particularly in England – have tended

to overlook the fact of Gerson's absence when England came to play Brazil. That is not to say that England didn't play thoroughly well, that they did not suggest themselves as one of the two or three best teams of the tournament during that game. It was a classic, worthy to enter the Pantheon of brilliant World Cup games. The English had gone to Mexico in the rôle of villains, with too many people disgruntled as to the manner of their victory four years earlier; and this animosity was to manifest itself at every turn. The night before the Brazil game a crowd several thousand strong milled round the Hilton Hotel, where they were staying, and contrived to make enough noise to prevent the players getting any sleep. Many admitted afterwards that they had for long minutes and hours simply stood by the windows of their rooms, staring at the crowd below, and at the inability of the Mexican police to deal with the problem.

They then went out at midday, in scorching heat that approached 100 degrees of Fahrenheit and played Brazil off the pitch for long stretches of the game. Mullery played brilliantly, policing Pelé with scrupulous toughness. True, Pelé got away from him in the early minutes of the game after Jairzinho had rounded Cooper on England's left and smacked across a perfect centre; up went Pelé, down came the ball, and down also came Gordon Banks to scoop the ball up with his right wrist – a save that must rank with the very best in the history of the World Cup tournament. Otherwise Pelé was kept moderately quiet; and Moore at the heart of the defence gave further evidence that he was the best defensive player in the world, his timing of the tackle precise, his reading of the game astute, his distribution imaginative.

The only goal of the match (perfect evidence that goals in themselves do not exciting football make) came after fourteen minutes of the second half, after Tostao had teased the left of the English defence and slid the ball across goal for Jairzinho to score. The truth was, however, that if Banks was forced to at least three other saves of high quality, England were given, and missed, a plentitude of chances at the other end. Ball hit the bar, missed another good chance; Astle blazed wide after being put into an attractive position; Hurst might have had a goal, but shot feebly at the crucial moment. If the style is the man, then the style must also be the game; and yet again we were left to ponder that one of the essential weaknesses of the English game was its lack of high technical accomplishment – where the world's best strikers would snap up chances with glee, too often English forwards had not the basic 'killer' instinct that comes hand in hand (or foot to foot) with technical prowess.

The Brazilians went on to beat the Rumanians, again despite the deprivation of Gerson; and, on this occasion, that of Rivelino. England drafted in a handful of 'reserves' for the game against the Czechs, played badly, won through a disputed penalty; and joined Brazil in the quarter-finals.

In group IV were the mysterious Peruvians. In their first game, they fell behind to Bulgaria, conceded two goals from set pieces; and then in the second half turned on their skills. Many were quick to compare them with the Brazilians in their flamboyance, their brilliant control. In defence they had a sturdy player in Chumpitaz, some imaginative forwards in Gallardo, Sotil, Cubillas and Baylon; and in the space of twenty minutes turned the two-goal deficit into a 3-2 score that would last until the game's finish.

That would prove to be the decisive game in the group. For although they fared poorly against Morocco in their first match, the West Germans seemed certainties for qualification; a thought that was reinforced when they came to play the Bulgarians in turn. Though the East Europeans scored first through Nikodimov (following a free kick), the Germans ran in five goals, three of them going to Muller. Libuda was on venomous form on their right, Muller and Seeler brave and energetic in the middle. In fact Muller would score another hat trick when the Germans came to meet Peru a few days later, marching firmly along the road that would make him the tournament's highest scorer. Despite that 3-1 defeat, Peru would qualify.

No goal Muller scored in the competition was, however, more important than that he slashed home in the quarter-final tie that followed, when the Germans were drawn against England. It was a game England could, and should, have won. For a team of their defensive prowess to lead by two clear goals and eventually lose by the odd score in five was remarkable. It is too easy to blame Peter Bonetti, drafted into the goalkeeping position after Banks had been forced to withdraw with a stomach complaint of mysterious origin. Banks may well have saved two of the three German goals to be scored; but there were other, better reasons to explain the collapse.

England's lead came through Mullery – racing through to exchange passes with Lee, sliding the ball out to Newton on the right, smashing home the perfect cross; and Peters – knocking in another fine cross from Newton. That left England two up after five minutes of the second half, and seemingly set for a good win. And then came the substitutions – Grabowski on for Libuda; Bell and Hunter on for Charlton and Peters – that were to prove decisive. While Charlton remained, Beckenbauer, his policeman, stayed quiet; without further patrolling duties, Beckenbauer cut loose, scored the first, important, German goal. Where Cooper had controlled Libuda on the left, he now found Grabowski irrepressible. Although Hurst nearly made the score 3-1 with a fine low header, it was the Germans who came through, Seeler backheading a long cross from Schnellinger.

As in the 1966 Final, the game between the two countries entered extra time, with the crowd noisily pro-German, and England's defence looking increasingly tired. Hurst scored – to be given, mysteriously, offside. And then came the deciding goal – Grabowski winning control on the right, punting over a cross, which Muller tucked away as the ball was nodded down to him. England were out of the competition, after having controlled vast stretches of their games against Brazil and West Germany, after having suggested themselves strongly as possible opposition for Brazil in the Final.

Through into the semi-finals with Germany would go Italy, Brazil and Uruguay. The last won through in the final moments of extra time in a hard game against the Russians, and with a hotly disputed goal into the bargain. But the Russians had missed too many chances to have reason for bitter complaint.

Brazil went through, now with both Rivelino and Gerson back in the side, and at the expense of Peru to the tune of 4-2. Gallardo scored two goals for the entertaining Peruvians, but they were up against a side that knew their own footballing language and were more adept practitioners.

And Italy went through, stuttering for much of their game against Mexico, until Gianni Rivera made his appearance at the start of the second half and suggested openings for his compatriots. Riva scored twice, delighting those who knew his prowess and were still waiting patiently for evidence of its existence; and there was a goal from Rivera himself, nice ammunition for those who felt that Italy were squandering his exquisite talents, that there should always have been a place for him in that team, with or without the brave resourceful Sandro Mazzola.

The semi-final draw – Brazil against Uruguay, Italy against West Germany – promised, and delivered, much. The first of these games pitted the resource of the Brazilian midfield and attack against the misanthropy of the Uruguayan defence, with its squad of muscular central defenders. In the event, it was Uruguay who scored first, through Cubilla (as opposed to Cubillas, the Peruvian), and though Brazil equalised just before half time through Clodoaldo, the important second goal did not materialise until fourteen minutes before the end, when Jairzinho danced past three defenders on the right and drove the ball home from a sharp angle. A goal from Rivelino in the last second of the game gave the scoreline a lopsided quality that was grossly unfair to the courage and ingenuity of much of the Uruguayan play, still deprived of the skills of the injured – and potentially influential – Pedro Rocha.

But Italy against West Germany – that was really something of a collector's item. It was an interesting comment on the Italian footballing mentality that after a game of thrilling interest, despite the fact that their team had been victorious, many Italian commentators would dismiss it as being something of a circus turn on the grounds that neither of the two defences was good enough. In fact, Italy created much of their good fortune early in the game when a bad tackle by Bertini left the elegant Beckenbauer with an injured arm. He would play much of the game at strolling pace and in some pain, his arm strapped to his chest.

The Italians took the lead after only seven minutes, Boninsegna clearing Riva out of his way to plant a left-footed shot firmly past Maier. Given the Italian penchant for defensive expertise, the Germans must have known that they had a titanic struggle on their hands, and well though they played against the cautious Italians in the second half, too many chances went begging. Indeed it was not until the third minute of injury time that Schnellinger, the German sweeper (and ironically he served brilliantly in that rôle at club level for A.C. Milan), came forward to slide the ball home after Grabowski had crossed from the left.

Into extra-time, and on came the nervousness and the mistakes. The Germans went ahead after five minutes through Muller; Burgnich came up to knock in Rivera's free kick; Riva scored a fine goal with that formidable left foot of his – and the first period of extra-time ended with Italy leading 3-2. The Italians were pulled back again soon after the resumption of play, when Muller dived low to head home; and then came the decisive goal, with the talented Boninsegna taking the ball out to the left, leaving his opponent Schulz on his bottom, and crossing for Gianni Rivera to drive the ball precisely into goal. Once again Rivera had missed the first forty-five minutes; once again he had been decisive in the later stages of a game. The Italians were through, not remotely the second best side in the tournament, but undoubtedly one of high technical accomplishment, and in that semi-final game, having given the lie to those detractors eager to claim that Italian teams always lack fire and spirit.

In the play-off for third place the Germans did what the Italians had failed to do – and beat Uruguay. They did so with a fine goal scored by Overath after a thrilling movement that involved Libuda, Muller and Seeler. There was entertaining action at both ends, with Mazurkiewicz and Walter (the young German goalkeeper) both being forced to fine saves. But a match of technical adroitness could not raise the crowd – which, like the televised world, awaited the Final itself.

Brazil won it, and won it handsomely. They did so with football of assured fluency, they did it by underlining brilliantly, and against the master exponents of defensive football, all the old clichés about attack being the best means of defence. Of the Italians Sandro Mazzola covered vast tracts of ground, played with authority and spirit; Boninsegna showed what a dangerous striker he could be, given even a few metres of space; Facchetti strove manfully against Jairzinho. But much of the marking was sloppy on the one hand, crude on the other; and there was about the team as a whole a curious refusal to play with any real vestige of self-confidence.

It was, fittingly, Pelé who gave the Brazilians the lead after eighteen minutes, heading down Rivelino's cross; if the great man had a comparatively human game, then his presence and brilliance had given the tournament as a whole a fine streak of class. And no one looked more bemused than he when the Italians equalised a few minutes before half-time through Boninsegna and after a silly back-pass by Clodoaldo had left Felix stranded outside the Brazilian goal.

That was delusion indeed, for in the second half, the Brazilians made heavy amends. Gerson, who throughout played with a majesty that capitalised on the failure of the Italian midfield, was the scorer of the second of the four Brazilian goals, his left foot curling in a fine shot from distance. Jairzinho it was who scored the third, slipping in a pass from Pelé and setting a new record by virtue of having scored in all six games in which he played; and the Italians were a thoroughly demoralised side by the time Carlos Alberto came through down the right touchline to crash the ball in after an exquisitely weighted pass from Pelé had put him through in the last few minutes of the game.

The Italians brought on Juliano for the ineffectual Bertini; with six minutes to go, bizarrely substituted Rivera for Boninsegna – a move that was staggering in its lack of logic. Had Rivera appeared earlier, in place of the tired Domenghini, one might have seen the point, he might have effected something of a rescue. But the ship had been truly sunk; despite their appearance in the Final the Italians would go home and indulge in the most Machiavellian post-mortems. And by virtue of their third victory, the Brazilians would appropriate the Jules Rimet trophy.

It was a popular victory, a welcome evidence that attacking football and intuitive genius still had their place in a footballing world obsessed by 'work-rate' and (often) skill-less hard running. Winning the tournament in 1966 England had conceded only three goals, scored eleven. Four years later, the Brazilians had triumphed by conceding seven goals and scoring nineteen. Either England or West Germany – not to mention Uruguay – might have made of the Final more than did the Italians. And it remained true (as it may always remain true) that some of the refereeing left much to be desired. But Ferenc Puskas, and many other great stars of the past, would have approved. The football of the Brazilians was many miles removed from the 'war' that people had gloomily forecast as being the only result of international competition. Above all, the Brazilians made the thing look enjoyable, had helped to restore that enthusiasm without which sport in any form will wither away. More chants of '*samba*', and the spectacle of the greatest player of that, or any, generation – Pelé – being raised aloft by delighted Brazilian fans.

1970 – Final Stages

Quarter-Finals

WEST GERMANY 3, ENGLAND 2 (0-1) (2-2) after extra time. *Leon*

WEST GERMANY: Maier; Schnellinger, Vogts, Fichtel, Hottges (Schulz); Beckenbauer, Overath, Seeler; Libuda (Grabowski), Muller, Loehr.

ENGLAND: Bonetti (Chelsea); Newton (Everton); Cooper (Leeds United); Mullery (Spurs), Labone (Everton), Moore

(West Ham United); Lee (Manchester City), Ball (Everton), Hurst (West Ham United), Charlton (Manchester United) [Bell (Manchester City)], Peters (Spurs) [Hunter (Leeds United)].
SCORERS: Mullery, Peters for England; Beckenbauer, Seeler, Muller for West Germany.

BRAZIL 4, PERU 2 (2-1). *Guadalajara*

BRAZIL: Felix; Carlos Alberto, Brito, Piazza, Marco Antonio; Clodoaldo, Gerson (Paulo Cesar); Jairzinho (Roberto), Tostao, Pelé, Rivelino.
PERU: Rubiños; Campos, Fernandez, Chumpitaz, Fuentes; Mifflin, Challe; Baylon (Sotil), Perico Leon (Eladio Reyes), Cubillas, Gallardo.
SCORERS: Rivelino, Tostao (2), Jairzinho for Brazil; Gallardo, Cubillas for Peru.

ITALY 4, MEXICO 1 (1-1). *Toluca*

ITALY: Albertosi; Burgnich, Cera, Rosato, Facchetti; Bertini, Mazzola (Rivera), De Sisti; Domenghini (Gori), Boninsegna, Riva.
MEXICO: Calderon; Vantolra, Pena, Guzman, Perez; Gonzales (Borja), Pulido, Munguia (Diaz); Valdivia, Fragoso, Padilla.
SCORERS: Domenghini, Riva (2), Rivera for Italy; Gonzales for Mexico.

URUGUAY 1, RUSSIA 0 (0-0) after extra time. *Mexico*

URUGUAY: Mazurkiewicz; Ubinas, Ancheta, Matosas, Mujica; Maneiro, Cortes, Montero Castillo; Cubilla, Fontes (Gomez), Morales (Esparrago).
RUSSIA: Kavazashvili; Dzodzuashvili, Afonin, Khurtsilava (Logofet), Chesternijev; Muntijan, Asatiani (Kiselev), Kaplichni; Evriuzhkinzin, Bychevetz, Khmelnitzki.
SCORER: Esparrago for Uruguay.

Semi-Finals

ITALY 4, WEST GERMANY 3 (1-0) (1-1) after extra time. *Mexico City*

ITALY: Albertosi; Cera; Burgnich, Bertini, Rosato, (Poletti) Facchetti; Domenghini, Mazzola (Rivera), De Sisti; Boninsegna, Riva.
WEST GERMANY: Maier; Schnellinger; Vogts, Schulz, Beckenbauer, Patzke; Seeler, Overath; Grabowski, Muller, Loehr (Libuda).
SCORERS: Boninsenga, Burgnich, Riva, Rivera, for Italy; Schnellinger, Muller (2) for West Germany.

BRAZIL 3, URUGUAY 1 (1-1). *Guadalajara*

BRAZIL: Felix; Carlos Alberto, Brito, Piazza, Everaldo; Clodoaldo, Gerson; Jairzinho, Tostao, Pelé, Rivelino.
URUGUAY: Mazurkiewicz; Ubinas, Ancheta, Matosas, Mujica; Montero Castillo, Cortes, Fontes; Cubilla, Maneiro (Esparrago), Morales.
SCORERS: Cubilla for Uruguay; Clodoaldo, Jairzinho, Rivelino for Brazil.

Third Place Match

WEST GERMANY 1, URUGUAY 0 (1-0). *Mexico City*
WEST GERMANY: Walter, Schnellinger (Lorenz); Patzke, Fichtel, Weber, Vogts; Seeler, Overath; Libuda (Loehr), Muller, Held.
URUGUAY: Mazurkiewicz; Ubinas, Ancheta, Matosas, Mujica; Montero Castillo, Cortes, Fontes (Sandoval); Cubilla, Maneiro (Esparrago), Morales.
SCORER: Overath for West Germany.

Final

BRAZIL 4, ITALY 1 (1-1). *Mexico City*

BRAZIL: Felix; Carlos Alberto, Brito, Piazza, Everaldo; Clodoaldo, Gerson; Jairzinho, Tostao, Pelé, Rivelino.
ITALY: Albertosi; Cera; Burgnich, Bertini, (Juliano), Rosato, Facchetti; Domenghini, Mazzola, De Sisti; Boninsegna (Rivera), Riva.
SCORERS: Pelé, Gerson, Jairzinho, Carlos Alberto for Brazil; Boninsegna for Italy.

3 VICTORIOUS WEST GERMANY – AT LAST (1974)

World Cup 1974 – held in West Germany

Finalists in 1966; third in 1970: Winners of the European Nations Championship in 1972 – when they played their most skilful and fluid football – this triumph of being the winning side in the World Cup of 1974 was a very fitting 'finale' to a decade in which West Germany had always been at, or near, the top. I say 'finale' being very aware of their record in the 1976 European Nations Championship when they played in the Final – only losing to Czechoslovakia on penalty kicks after the two teams had finished playing a period of 'extra time' and finishing equal. A marvellously successful record.

For the first time since 1950 the knock-out element would be partly discarded. The teams would still play in four groups, but the top two teams in each group would go on to play, not the quarter-final stage but in two further groups – the winners of such groups to play each other in the Final and the teams who finished second to play each other for third and fourth places.

The footballing world was stunned by the failure of England to qualify. Winners in 1966, one of the two or three best teams in 1970 – their failure to qualify showed how slender the margin between success and failure in the game could be: and how large a part could be played by sheer good fortune.

England were drawn in a group with Wales and Poland – who had been the Olympic champions two years previously. Despite that they were not thought to pose a great threat to England, whose first game in their group was in Cardiff – where they won by the only goal of the match, scored by Bell.

That seemed to make the return game, at Wembley, a mere formality for the English. But Wales scored first, through Toshack; and though England scored an equalising goal, they could not score again. A result that would prove to do no good to either side!

England travelled to Poland in June 1973, dropped a forward (Channon) and replaced him with a defender (Storey) and, playing with a certain amount of clumsiness, lost 2-0. They had given a further warning as to the grit and the flair of Poland.

When the Poles came to Wembley in the October of 1973, the English could not but be pleased that the star centre-forward of Poland, Lubanski, had to miss the game on account of injury. It was a game England simply had to win in order to qualify for the final tournament – and they had to watch Poland score first, through Domarski. They came back at Poland through a penalty scored by Clarke; but try as they might (and they appeared to try everything) they could not score another goal. The goalkeeper for Poland, Tomaszewski, was all arms and legs, halted every shot the English fired at him. (And in the competition proper he seemed to have further great strokes of luck!) In the words of the Italian team manager, Enzo Bearzot, 'the Poles went to the last World Cup and could have won it, yet at Wembley they were lucky not to give away seven goals'. Maybe if Hector – a player whose great strength lay on his left side – had been brought on earlier, the havoc caused on the right side of the Polish defence may have led to some goals.

England had the consolation of going out to a side whose exploits would thrill the world of football. Their midfield player, Deyna, would be widely admired throughout the world as being the most influential of stars, a very cunning strategist; Lato, who had taken over from the injured Lubanski the gift of being in the right place at the right time, would become the leading scorer of the tournament; the huge Gorgon would become a central defender widely admired; and Tomaszewski would go on to play some great games, showing that no little skill went hand-in-hand with his good fortune.

For the first time since they had entered the competition – in 1950 – England had failed to qualify for the final stages of a World Cup tournament. On February 14 an enquiry began into the 'whys' and 'wherefores' of the defeat against Poland; and on May 1 a statement was issued saying that Sir Alf Ramsey had been asked to resign, had refused and therefore had been given his dismissal. The timing seemed strange. In April Ramsey had taken a team to Portugal – before beginning a series of seven matches – for which games he had already picked a squad! First came the Home International Tournament, with a game against Scotland – already through to the final stage of the World Cup; then a game at Wembley against Argentina – playing a number of games on their way to West Germany; then a tour around Eastern Europe – against teams who had all qualified for the World Cup finals! So, of the seven matches, five were against teams who would go to West Germany; Bulgaria were beaten, the only loss was that against Scotland, and the other three games were drawn: against Argentina, Yugoslavia and East Germany, all teams who qualified to play in the Second Round of the tournament! Joe Mercer had the good fortune to be 'stop-gap' manager of this squad, while the search went on for a coach on a permanent basis.

In total, the ten-year record under Ramsey was good: played 113, won 69, drawn 27, lost 17. But England teams had often been 'hard to beat' instead of packed with gifted players: which has been, with a few exceptions, true of English football in general in the past few years.

Wales had been doomed earlier than England – but at least had the small satisfaction of having beaten Poland at Cardiff. And Northern Ireland, for their part, had never looked like qualifying – being drawn in a group with Bulgaria, Portugal and Cyprus. In fact the only points Cyprus obtained was in their home defeat of Northern Ireland.

Scotland were drawn in a group which contained Czechoslovakia and Denmark. Tommy Docherty had gone southwards, after taking Scotland to wins over Denmark – at home and away; leaving in his place Willie Ormond. In his first game as manager his team took a 5-0 drubbing at home to England – and that in a special memorial match on St Valentine's Day! Then, two months later, his team lost at home to Northern Ireland. But all became good before they played their home game against Czechoslovakia – for they learned the Czechs had been held to a draw when they travelled to play in Denmark. They won through by the score of 2-1, thanks to goals from two men – Holton and Morgan – from the team Docherty had gone southwards to manage: Manchester United!

Of the other European nations, the following also qualified: Sweden (after a play-off match with Austria); Italy (after playing a scoreless draw at Naples with visiting Turkey); Holland (edging out the hapless Belgium on goal difference, the Belgians not having lost a match nor conceded a goal); East Germany – in the final stages of the tournament for the first time; Bulgaria and Yugoslavia. Russia won through from its group, played Chile in Moscow – and refused to play the return leg for reasons more political than sporting! Chile, therefore, won a place in the tournament proper.

Brazil, as holders, won their place automatically; as did the 'host' country – West Germany. The other teams to qualify from South America were Argentina; Uruguay (who beat

Colombia on goal difference); and, as we have seen, Chile – having beaten on their way Peru, who had played so excitingly in Mexico four years earlier.

Zaire qualified from Africa – and played throughout with an enthusiasm that went some way towards hiding their lack of skill; Australia won their way through from the groups covered by Asian teams – and countries from the Pacific coast; and from the zone of 'North and Central America' qualified Haiti. So for teams from Morocco, El Salvador and Israel in 1970, read Zaire, Haiti and Australia for 1974.

A few points to wonder about before we begin a run-down of the matches. The team who gave most pleasure, many people thought, was Holland. West Germany, for its part, had many uncomfortable moments in the games from the Second Round, particularly against Sweden and Poland (where they were to a major extent 'saved' by some very effective work in goal by Maier). And, of course, the West Germans had a few nasty moments in their group games – in the opening match against Chile, and their loss against the East Germans, even though they had already been sure of qualifying. This 'failure' to qualify indeed worked very well for them in the fact that they thus moved into the Second Section; and, most importantly, ensured that they would not meet Holland before – and, of course, if – they qualified for the Final or the match to decide the third place.

This Holland team was thought by many 'experts' to be on a par with that team of Brazil's – which won the trophy in 1958, 1962 and 1970. In players such as Cruyff, Neeskens, Krol and Van Hanegem the side had players brilliant enough to play for an eleven drawn from the best in the world. Why, you rightly enquire, did they not beat West Germany in the Final? Partly because they had become so used to winning their games – sometimes by huge scores; partly, because they met in the West German team one that was given a massively loud support from its home crowd, always willing it on towards victory; and partly, because for the first time in recent years, man-to-man marking of Cruyff (by Vogts) worked marvellously well.

European teams did much better than their South American counterparts: picking up, for a start, the first three places. In total the table looks like this:

1 West Germany	9 Scotland
2 Holland	10 Italy
3 Poland	11 Chile
4 Brazil	12 Bulgaria
5 Sweden	13 Uruguay
6 East Germany	14 Australia
7 Yugoslavia	15 Haiti
8 Argentina	16 Zaire

And the only time a South American team beat a European team was when Brazil beat East Germany in a game from the Second Section.

The reasons for this pitiful decline are many, but the casual physical preparation of the teams from South America was an effect. With no outstanding team of forwards, they huddled up much more in defence – at which they have for long been less gifted than their European counterparts. And their play seemed strangely 'old-fashioned' at a time when Europe had a near-glut of teams prepared to try new ideas, to play with new concepts.

Ninety-seven goals were scored in the thirty-eight matches – an average of 2·7 per match. But take away the twenty-eight goals conceded by Zaire and Haiti and you are left with an average of pitifully near two per game. Sombre thought.

Some quite strict refereeing came into force; thereby helping to quell any explosions of violence. Only five players were sent off the pitch: Caszely of Chile, Richards of Australia, Ndaye of Zaire, Luis Pereira of Brazil and Julio Montero Castillo of Uruguay. And some of the best refereeing came from Babacan of Turkey, Barreto of Uruguay, Suppiah of Singapore, Clive Thomas of Wales and Jack Taylor – who controlled the Final both bravely and perceptively – of England.

The first game to be played, as always, allowed us to have a good look at the holders – Brazil. Their competitors on the opening day were Yugoslavia; and the group from which they both came, Group II, proved to be the tightest group, with Zaire and Scotland involved as well. For the third time successively, the tournament began with a goalless draw. The Brazilians appeared to be much more aware of their defence than previously, had fewer gifted runners in attack; while for Yugoslavia, we were given an early look at the midfield player, Oblak, who proved to be a planner of guile and quickness.

Scotland were drawn in that group against a team no one knew much about: Zaire. 30,000 came to find out on the next day; and Willie Ormond, the Scotland team manager, gave a World Cup game to Denis Law. He and Jordan won a vast amount of the ball from the air, and brought it down to the feet of Lorimer. Indeed Lorimer scored first in the twenty-sixth minute, and Jordan scored the second six minutes later. But try as they might – and they tried nearly everything – Scotland could score no more in the fifty-eight minutes that remained, a failure that was eventually to prove decisive.

Yugoslavia showed how to do it four days later – putting nine into the Zaire goal in the match. Four goals had gone in when the goalkeeper was substituted in the twenty-third minute. And a somewhat pitiful incident occurred in this match when a defender from the Zaire team, called Mwepu, aimed a kick at the referee's backside; and watched with relief while the referee sent off Ndaye, who had been a spectator of the crime all along! On the same day Scotland drew a goalless game with Brazil. They played for seventy-five per cent of the match in the Brazilian half, led superbly in midfield by Billy Bremner. He seemed to cover vast areas of the field with his determined running, very ably helped, as the match progressed, by David Hay. Among the forwards both Lorimer and Morgan had busy matches; and in defence the strong tackling and running of both Holton and Buchan did much to make the powerful running of the much-feared Jairzinho – top scorer in the tournament four years previously – null and void. Many people who saw the game thought the Scots desperately unlucky not to score one or two goals.

So Scotland went into the next game needing to win; or hoping against hope Brazil would win by less than two goals in their game against Zaire. With the two games taking place at the same time, things looked promising at half-time for Scotland. There was no score in the game between Scotland and Yugoslavia; and the Brazilians, who had been through two scoreless games, found it hard to add to a goal scored by Jairzinho in the first half. But half-way through the second half Rivelino, with a screaming drive from twenty-five metres, changed things; and soon after Brazil achieved their third goal from Valdomiro. Scotland now had to win; and the chances of that happening were much diminished when Yugoslavia went ahead, with a goal scored by the substitute Karasi. And although Joe Jordan acquired the equaliser, there was no time for Scotland to add to that. Scotland, the only team to remain undefeated in this World Cup, had to watch themselves being eliminated on goal difference. They must surely have rued not scoring more goals in their first game! The Scotland players who competed in this tournament were: Harvey in goal; Jardine, McGrain, Holton, Blackley and Buchan in defence; Bremner, Hay, Dalglish and Hutchison in midfield; Law, Morgan, Lorimer and Jordan in attack.

In Group I it soon became apparent that everything was going to hinge on the game between the German sides, playing each other for the first time since the rift over twenty years earlier. But there were some surprises en route. West Germany defeated Chile by a single goal scored by Breitner; but not before Chile had given them some frights with the German team looking very far from composed in midfield and attack. That was in Berlin and on the same day in Hamburg, East Germany had to use some violence in their game with Australia: no less than three of their players being shown the yellow card! Their goals (one an own-goal by Curran!) came in the second half. Alston had shown himself to be a striker of promise, Bulgevic an incisive runner on the wing and Wilson a calm and authoritative 'sweeper'.

Four days later East Germany had been held to a draw by Chile; who in many respects showed themselves to be much more at ease than their opponents. In Reinoso they had a midfield player of speed and intelligence; in Figueroa they possessed one of the best defenders in the tournament, almost always an impenetrable barrier. The scores came in the second half; Hoffman scoring from a rebound from a Ducke free-kick and Ahumada turning in a cross from the best player on the field, Reinoso.

On the same day West Germany put three goals past Reilly, the Australian goalkeeper. For the Germans Overath, Beckenbauer and Hoeness were the best players; and for the Australians Alston as striker and Wilson as sweeper again had good games, Reilly made some courageous saves in goal. In their next match, against Chile, the Australians experienced nearly everything: torrential rain (which held up the match) a political demonstration – ending up with the police arresting several supporters, and with a banner being placed across the pitch. The game was yet another scoreless draw, with many chances at either end, particularly for Australia, when Alston gave Abonyi a chance, which the latter squandered. But once more Alston, Buljevic and Wilson showed themselves to be players of some skill. A curious thing in the game was the dismissal of Richards, the midfield player for Australia who stayed on the field for perhaps five minutes after receiving his second yellow card from the referee; and going off only when the linesman drew the referee's attention to the law concerning dimissals.

And so the game between the two Germanies – and the only appearance of Gunther Netzer, who had played such an important part in the German triumph of the European Nations Cup victory two years earlier. Some cynics might accuse the West Germans of not trying too hard to win, and therefore avoiding playing the more fancied Holland in the Second round; and they might have possibly been aware that in their previous triumph in this competition in 1954 they had also lost a match in their group, to the team from Hungary, which – quixotically – they were to play and beat in the Final.

Group III saw the team many people favoured, Holland. A team from Holland had not played in the final tournament for many years, but the way their leading club sides had strolled through European club competitions in recent years had given many people much excitement and they were strongly favoured to perform well in national competition. On the first day of their competition they showed how abysmally Uruguay had fallen from their achievement four years previously, when they had been semi-finalists. From the start the players from South America fell back in defence, and committed foul after foul. Three Uruguayan players were booked and Julio Montero Castillo was sent off for aiming a series of knee-high tackles. The only Uruguayan players to show some skill were Mazurkiewicz in goal and Pedro Rocha in midfield. The two Holland goals were scored by Johnny Rep.

Holland next played a goalless draw against Sweden, Johan Cruyff directing operations for them, and for Sweden Hellstroem in goal looking a very good, safe and acrobatic player, and up front the tall Edstroem seeming to be a player of the highest class. On the same day Uruguay, a team with no fighting spirit and a paucity of skill, drew 1-1 with Bulgaria. Holland, four days later, played superbly to defeat Bulgaria 4-1: the goal 'against' being an own-goal and the only goal Jongbloed would concede until the Final! And on the same day, Sweden would beat Uruguay 3-0, the tall Edstroem scoring twice. Before the Uruguay team left West Germany their manager, Roberto Porta, was on record as having said: 'This is the worst football we have ever played. It is a national disgrace: we shall be tried publicly on our return.' So – Holland and Sweden were the teams to go through to the Second Round.

Group IV moved along very peaceably, there being no rough play when Italy, Poland and Argentina met each other. The first game from this group saw Italy playing Haiti; and when the Haiti team scored just after the interval through Sanon, the first goal to be conceded for 1,143 minutes by Zoff in the Italian goal, the crowd must have begun to wonder whether the misfortune that the Italian teams appear to visit upon themselves had yet again come to pass. But the ghost of North Korea had been partly laid to rest in Mexico, and Italy ended the game by being 3-1 victors; although the Haiti goalkeeper, Francillon was to make a series of extraordinary saves – and stayed on in West Germany to play for the club side of Munich 1860. Mazzola, for Italy, was very industrious; a good thing too, knowing the Italian technique of playing matches on paper before playing them for real. A saddening footnote, however. Ernst Jean-Joseph, a Haiti defender, was found to have taken drugs before the match, was beaten up and sent home in disgrace on the orders of Duvalier, the son of 'Papa' Doc.

The other game played on June 15 was between Poland and Argentina, the former beating a spirited Argentinian side 3-2, having scored twice in the first ten minutes. As the match went on, Argentina came to play more strongly, thereby going in the face of those who thought they had been badly-prepared and were too 'frail'! Lato scored two goals, making a good start in his successful attempt to become the leading scorer of the tournament.

Poland's next trick was to show how easy it was to beat Haiti by running in seven goals against them on the following Wednesday. But Francillon, in goal, had another fine game and but for some very acrobatic saves from him the score would comfortably have been in double figures. And on the same day Italy could get no more than a draw from Argentina; the Italian 'goal' being a score against his own side by Perfumo, their sweeper who played with great composure in the tournament of 1966.

Their 50,000 supporters in the crowd of 70,000 made a tremendous racket but cheers soon turned to whistles of despair when the 'Squadra' began to play badly. Houseman's scoring shot from thirty metres came after he had played a beautiful 'scissors' move with his midfield companion, Babington. For Italy Riva and Rivera had poor matches; but Mazzola always ran purposefully and made some telling passes. So they went into the match against Poland needing just a draw to be sure of making further progress.

Alas, it was not to be. Their main striker 'Gigi' Riva, was ruled out through injury; and they left out Rivera. Their support turned out as numerically strong as before; but had very little to cheer. The score was Poland 2 Italy 1; and the Italian goal from Capello didn't come before the eight-sixth minute – a repeat of that game eight months earlier when Italy had come to Wembley and achieved a win in the same minute! But this time they were well beaten; Szarmach scoring first, when he turned in a very narrow space, and Deyna scoring before the interval, driving home a cross from Kasperczak. For Italy, Mazzola seemed to run everywhere; but it was Deyna who was the best player on view – and with Kasperczak and Maszczyk formed a very thrilling midfield. After their dismissal from the competition of 1966 the Italian team were forced to dodge some flying tomatoes; but this time the team were attacked by some 500 'supporters' as they left the pitch in Stuttgart. *Povera Squadra Azzura*!

In the first of the groups in the Second Section were Argentina, Holland, Brazil and East Germany – apart from Holland the 'medium' sides; and in the other, stronger group were Yugoslavia, Sweden, Poland and West Germany.

Holland began by defeating Argentina by 4-0, in a glorious display of attacking football. Cruyff was on sensationally good form, scoring a goal in each half; the other goals coming from Krol and Rep. On this day there seemed to be little point in trying to mark certain players, when defenders ran as swiftly as forwards and when Holland played a type of 'Total Football' – forwards and defenders linking smoothly together in any part of the field. On the same day Brazil beat East Germany by the one goal, scored by Rivelino who had a glorious game in midfield for his team.

He also scored in the next game, in which Brazil beat Argentina 2-1, his shot going in from twenty-five metres, Carnevali, in the opposing goal, being obstructed by his defenders. The other goals came from Jairzinho and Brindisi – the first goal to be conceded by Brazil in this tournament.

They next encountered Holland, and were given a very sharp lesson in footballing skill. Their central defender, Luis Pereira, was sent off the field for having committed a scything chop on Neeskens; and this came after Ze Maria had perpetrated a rugby tackle on Cruyff, and the other central defender from Brazil, Mario Marinho, had assaulted Neeskens off the ball. In fact the entire team for Holland deserve to be praised for keeping their heads calm, while the Brazil players were losing theirs. Following their 2-0 defeat, attempts were made to burn down the house of their manager, Zagalo; and coffins for their leading players were paraded in the streets. So from this group Holland came out first again undefeated; and Brazil came out second.

In Group B West Germany got off to a brisk start by defeating Yugoslavia 2-0, their goals coming from Breitner (again!) in the first half and the inevitable Muller in the second. And on the same day the teams West Germany would find hard to beat, Poland and Sweden, were to play each other, Poland winning 1-0; with Tomaszewski having another fine day of good fortune in goal, and Lato scoring the goal and setting up scoring chances. Many people thought Sweden unfortunate not to force a draw.

Four days later, in Dusseldorf, West Germany beat Sweden 4-2. It was, despite a torrential downfall of rain, a match of the highest class. The Swedes scored first – a looping volley from the tall Edstroem: so Sweden led at half-time. Shortly after the interval came three goals in as many minutes: first Overath then Muller for the Germans, and then a goal by Sandberg for Sweden. Then two more, first a shot by Grabowski, then a penalty, awarded after Muller had been 'sandwiched' in the final minute, scored by Hoeness.

Three days later, West Germany were very fortunate not to be held to at least a draw by Poland. They won by a single goal, scored half-way through the second half. Many people were of the opinion that the match should have been postponed since it had rained very heavily in the morning, and the groundsmen had been kept extremely busy trying to make the surface playable by actually using towels to mop up the water. If the game had been delayed twenty-four hours, the extreme skill of the Poland midfield player, Deyna (maybe the most effective midfield player of the tournament) would have made itself felt. Muller (inevitably) scored the German goal after Tomaszewski (again inevitably!) saved a weakly-hit penalty by Hoeness. West

Germany to play the Final, against Holland; and Poland to play Brazil in the third place match.

So, on the day before the Final, Poland gained the reward (slight, I agree) of beating Brazil 1-0, the goal coming from Lato. This was not a Brazilian team such as the one that won so convincingly in Mexico, packed with fine players of rare technique; this was a much more drab team, relying for effect on a strong defence and powerful running, rather than brilliant passing in midfield. They were thought to be unfortunate when a shot by Rivelino struck a post, and very unfortunate when their substitute Mirandinha was held back unfairly by Kasperczak, when inside the Poland penalty area. But the only goal in the game came from Lato, in the seventy-sixth minute; who was on brilliantly sharp form in the attack. But, all in all hardly a lively 'warm-up' match for the following day's Final. Although the achievement of Poland, qualifying for a World Cup final tournament for the first time for nearly forty years, and performing so well, made a deep impression on the footballing world.

The Final, on the following day, proved to be something of a triumph for Helmut Schoen, who had gained second place with his team in 1966, third place in 1970. He had clung to Wolfgang Overath in the midfield – although the crowds preferred the play of the more gifted, more romantic Gunther Netzer; he played two wingers in most matches, Jurgen Grabowski and Bernd Holzenbein, although the former only had rare moments of skill and the latter was a touch inexperienced; he got Uli Hoeness to work harder by dropping him for the start of a game; he had Cruyff man-to-man marked, although it had never been tried previously; and he had the Master Card of Gerd Muller as striker.

Holland were close favourites to win before the game started, very popular favourites after they had taken a lead in the first minute when Jack Taylor, courageously and correctly, gave Holland a penalty for a tackle on Cruyff by Hoeness. Neeskens drove it down the centre of the goal while Maier dived to his right. Holland had scored without a single touch of the ball by a German!

Holland tried to press home their advantage by passing the ball quickly from wing to wing, attempting to tire out the Germans. But as Helmut Schoen pointed out, this team may have lacked the flair of the team that won the European Nations Championship – with Gunther Netzer playing so well in midfield – in 1972, but the team now had much more resolution, and were able to withstand the Dutch tactics very well. The Germans, altogether much stronger physically and playing a system of man-to-man marking, had a piece of good fortune when they were awarded a penalty of their own in the twenty-fifth minute; taken by Breitner, following the feeble penalty-kick in the match against Poland which had been taken by Hoeness, whose shot had been saved. Breitner made no mistake. Gradually, it became clear that with Vogts doing such a fine piece of marking on Cruyff and with Beckenbauer and Schwarzenbeck doing such a good job in the middle of the defence, with Hoeness and the new young player of immense talent, Bonhof, controlling the midfield those previously much-feared attacks by Holland were not taking place – since the Holland forwards were being starved of good service. And then, in the forty-third minute came the deciding goal from – who else – but Muller! Taking a long clearance from the amazing Bonhof, Muller skilfully turned around almost 180° and placed his shot between two defenders and Jongbloed. So, 2-1 to West Germany at half-time. And that was the score at full-time, with Cruyff not able to shake Vogts off, with Rep shooting clumsily twice and with a shot by Neeskens being saved by Maier.

So West Germany won a trophy in which they had the sheer will to win, the strength, the method and the skill. They beat the team – Holland – that most people thought would be victors in the Final, and that had given a vast degree of pleasure to many lovers of the game; but who were finally beaten at the end of the road by the team more disciplined, the team with the irrepressible goal-poacher in Muller, the team who, on the day, had a brilliant piece of man-to-man marking done on Johan Cruyff by Bertie Vogts.

1974 – FINAL STAGES

Third Place Match

POLAND 1, BRAZIL 0 (0-0)

POLAND: Tomaszewski; Szymanowski, Gorgon, Zmuda, Musial; Maszczyk, Deyna, Kasperczak (Cmikiewicz); Lato, Szarmach (Kapka), Gadocha.
BRAZIL: Leao; Ze Maria, M. Marinho, Alfredo, F. Marinho; Rivelino, Paulo Cesar II, Ademir Da Guia (Mirandinha); Valdomiro, Jairzinho, Dirceu.
SCORER: Lato for Poland.

FINAL

WEST GERMANY 2, HOLLAND 1 (2-1)

WEST GERMANY: Maier; Vogts, Schwarzenbeck, Beckenbauer, Breitner; Hoeness, Overath, Bonhof; Grabowski, Muller, Holzenbein.
HOLLAND: Jongbloed; Suurbier, Haan, Rijsbergen (De Jong) Krol; Jansen, Van Hanegem, Neeskens; Rep, Cruyff, Rensenbrink (Van de Kerkhoff).
SCORERS: Breitner (penalty), Muller for West Germany; Neeskens (penalty) for Holland.

4 FOOTBALL ROUND THE WORLD

It must be obvious that football is played to the same rules throughout the world. But the rules are only the framework of the game, and what lies inside that framework varies considerably in terms of appeal, style and character from continent to continent, from country to country. As no two painters will put on the canvas exactly the same ideas, so no two teams play exactly the same when it comes to international competition.

There are similarities, of course. Climate is so important. From those countries used to wet weather that turns pitches into quagmires, it is optimism indeed to expect to see brilliant ball control. The premiums will lie in strength, in close teamwork, in sophisticated team tactics. Those countries used to heat, conversely, often produce ball-juggling players of extraordinary reflex. Go to Brazil and you will see at any time of day on the famous Copacabana beach outside Rio de Janeiro thousands of youngsters playing for hour after hour quite happily under the hot sun, and nearby there is a group of pitches where they play quite happily all through the night; and go to Italy or Spain or Portugal and you will see the same sort of skills displayed.

The process becomes self-perpetuating, naturally; so that young players try to emulate their seniors. But styles do, to a certain extent, reflect national characteristics and attitudes. Foreign visitors to Britain often find very amusing our obsession with the forming of queues: and there is much of the queue mentality about British football. The Italians have a reputation for being something of a peacock nation: all noise and bustle and considerable beauty; and this is reflected partly in its football, along with the fundamental sense of caution of the Italian character. The West German teams have a penchant for regimentation – but allow their players freedom to spread wide their talents. The performances in the teams from West Germany in the European Nations Championship of 1972 and the World Cup in 1974 perfectly underlined the strengths of football in West Germany.

Of course, those successes underlined something else – that great teams are formed around a nucleus of talented players. Just look at some of the most outstanding teams since the war, and the point is clearly underlined. The dazzlingly gifted sides from Hungary in the early Fifties had Puskas, Boszik, Kocsis, Hidegkuti and Grocsis; the Real Madrid club side that swept off with the European Cup five years running had Gento and the incomparable Di Stephano throughout, and at times players such as Puskas, Kopa, Rial and Del Sol; the Brazilians of 1958 and 1962 had Gilmar in goal, forwards such as Pelé, Didì and that greatest of dribblers – Garrincha, not to mention the ubiquitous Zagalo; the England team in 1966 had a superb goalkepeer in Banks, a peerless defender in Bobby Moore and in Bobby Charlton a midfield player of enormous technical skill and accomplishment: the Brazilian team in 1970 had a Pelê of great skills and to match him had found a midfield player of real poise and craft in Gerson and an attacker of vulpine quickness in Jairzinho; and the team from West Germany in 1974 had a 'sweeper' of class in Beckenbauer, a striker of great menace in Muller and a hard-working midfield player in Overath – preferred to the more talented Gunther Netzer, who had been so self-assured and powerful in the winning European Nations Championship side two years previously.

If the differences between teams and teams, players and players, countries and countries are sometimes acute, then one factor has come, unhappily, to weld together every type of football – the need for success, and its corollary, the need to make money. In the Preface we saw how the brilliant player from Holland – Johan Cruyff, had just signed a contract to play for his club F.C. Barcelona for a year that would bring him a salary of the equivalent of £375,000. And the last World Cup was replete with players giving their (sometimes extravagant) demands to their administrators for their payments to be received if they won the World Cup.

People, understandably, copy success. While Hungary dazzled the footballing world in the early Fifties and Real Madrid and Brazil (the only team to win the World Cup in a continent other than its own) played so exhilaratingly later in the decade – many coaches tried to copy their style of play and go out with teams bent on playing attacking football. But while Internazionale of Milan carried much before them during the Sixties using an ultra-defensive system built up around *catenaccio*, while England won the World Cup of 1966 with a seemingly insurmountable defence – then the footballing world, in imitation, slunk back into its shell. Then came the triumph of Brazil in 1970, the emergence of a finc West German national side, the victories of Ajax of Amsterdam and Bayern Munich in the European Cup – and immediately the cry was for 'total football'. It means what it says: defenders running forward into positions of attack, attackers running back to defend. Willy Meisl had said as much twenty years before in his famous book *Soccer Revolution*: 'That, then, is the hope – the hope that we shall see in this tournament the sort of football which lays skills and techniques over national differences. Perhaps by looking at some of the national teams we can understand one aspect of the thing – the other lies in the hands of the players, or of God.'

Though very well aware that all four teams from Britain are mathematically denied a presence in the next tournament – Scotland having been drawn in the same qualifying group as Wales – I've included them, partly to show how minimal has been the contribution of British soccer in this tournament and partly for interest.

Argentina

Football was introduced here by British residents of Buenos Aires at the end of the last century; but it was not until the arrival (in large numbers) of Italian immigrants early in this century, that the game really took hold of the public imagination. Indeed the parent has often been harsh on the child – for during both the Thirties and the Fifties, wealthy Italian clubs raided the football market in Argentina, and carried off many great players. And many great players of local fame have been sold to French and Spanish clubs – thereby helping to diminish the problem of massive inflation which has lately struck the country. Traditionally skilful and pleasing, local football – deprived of some 'star' players – has often degenerated into crude and too physical a style of play. Nevertheless, the present team should perform well in the competition and, perhaps, even win the World Cup. (see chapter 7).

World Cup achievement:

1930 – Second
1934 – Beaten in first round
1938 – Did not enter
1950 – Did not enter
1954 – Failed to qualify
1958 – Last in group
1962 – Third in group
1966 – Quarter-finalists
1970 – Failed to qualify
1974 – Second in qualifying group; last in group of the Second round

Brazil

Introduced by Britons, football in Brazil was truly developed by a Hungarian, Dori Kurschner, who got over the secret of team-work and tactics to add to natural flair. A country that has produced an army of magnificently talented players – ball-jugglers of genius, intuitive in their grasp of how the game should be played. Chief among these have been Leonidas – who named himself after a Greek hero, and played with bright brilliance before the war, famed the world over for his aerial bicycle kick; and after the war Garrincha and Pelé – the former world-famous for his dribbling skills and the latter world-famous for his elastic movements and sense of ball-control worthy of a juggler. Brazil now, have a very solid defence indeed, with perhaps seven or eight players worthy of playing for most sides; and with Rivelino still deadly in midfield, playing in his third World Cup they may increase their already formidable record of having played in every tournament and winning three times.

World Cup achievement:

1930 – Second in qualifying pool
1934 – Beaten in first qualifying round
1938 – Semi-finalists, third
1950 – Finalists
1954 – Quarter-finalists
1958 – Winners
1962 – Winners
1966 – Third in qualifying group
1970 – Winners
1974 – Semi-finalists, fourth

Eire

This will be their first appearance in a World Cup final competition. As with the team that represents Northern Ireland, Eire have had to choose teams that have been independent since 1950. The teams used to be picked by selection committees, until the appointment in 1969 of Mike Meegan as the first manager to be accorded the full rights of team selection. He kept the job for three years, to be succeeded by Liam Tuohy – one of whose first acts was to take the team to the mini-World Cup, held in Brazil in 1972 – and returned with two wins and the feeling that there was there the makings of a good side. He, in turn, was succeeded by the man who did much to bring that scheme to fruition, Johnny Giles. A very gifted midfield player with Leeds United, Giles won his first cap at the age of eighteen – when with Manchester United; and now holds the record number of caps.

His first game as manager of Eire was in November 1973, and against the team from Poland who had just put England out of the 1974 World Cup by holding them to a draw. Eire won the game 1–0; and from then on Giles thought the best way to run the team from a small country was like a club side. His style is simple – he never makes detailed notes on paper of the opposition, but all goes into his mind so that any team-talk is concise and to the point. He believes very much in keeping to simple things and making sure that they are well done. Above all he tries to communicate his sheer enjoyment of the game together with his deep care. Their group contained Bulgaria – who have taken part in the last four tournaments – and France, who have played with great skill and drive recently. And a nice aspect of their 1–0 defeat of France was the many aspects of 'total football'; with forwards such as Givens and Heighway falling back to defend, and defenders like the talented O'Leary coming forward to aid the attack.

England

The Football Association was founded in 1863 and the F.A. Cup introduced in 1871.

With regard to international football, England withdrew from FIFA after having made a protest about the professionalism that seemed rampant inside the officially amateur Olympic tournaments. That was in 1928, and they would remain outside until 1946 – having refused to accept an offer to compete in the tournament finals of 1938, that year being played in France. The characteristics of the game are its great vigour, its comparative lack of hysteria and its professionalism are qualities that were appreciated by Alf Ramsey in taking the team to the World Cup victory of 1966. Other countries caught up in terms of flair and tactics but football as played in England remains highly thought of in the world; and England went out in the tournaments of the European Nations Championship in both 1972 and 1976 to the teams who eventually won, first West Germany and then Czechoslovakia.

Despite some encouraging results from their summer tour, England, alas!, will be very fortunate to qualify for the 1978 World Cup. It is to be seen whether their chance of qualifying was helped or hindered by the resignation in mid-summer of their manager, Don Revie.

World Cup achievement:

1950 – Second in qualifying group
1954 – Quarter-finalists
1958 – Lost in play-off to decide team to go further
1962 – Quarter-finalists
1966 – Winners
1970 – Quarter-finalists
1974 – Failed to qualify

France

If England did much to promote the progress of modern football throughout the world, then France did much to conceive and spread the progress of the World Cup. But the country's record in the competition has been a bit disappointing; their best attempt so far being in the 1958 World Cup when they reached the semi-finals, going out to the eventual winners, Brazil. In that tournament France had a side who played with skill, elan and strength; with that superb player in midfield, Raymond Kopa, making opening after opening for his forward line – one of whom, Just Fontaine, finishing as the highest scorer in the tournament.

The new team, under Michel Hidalgo, has a player said to be almost as good as Kopa and Fontaine rolled into one, Michel Platini! Even allowing for the enthusiastic exaggeration Platini has a very wide vision of the game, and is a runner of great speed with the happy knack of being close to goal at the right moment. Batheney in midfield and both Rocheteau and Rouyer in attack are players of great promise. France, like Eire, appear to have been harshly treated by quixotic refereeing in Bulgaria but should qualify for Argentina where this young team should do well.

World Cup achievement:

1930 – Beaten in qualifying group
1934 – Beaten in First Round
1938 – Beaten in Second Round
1950 – Withdrew after being invited to compete
1954 – Beaten in qualifying group
1958 – Semi-finalists
1962 – Did not qualify
1966 – Beaten in qualifying group
1970 – Did not qualify
1974 – Did not qualify

Holland

No team in a World Cup final tournament between 1938 and 1974. That is the strange truth about the football of Holland. Although football in Holland appeared on the scene at the beginning of the century, under the influence of British coaches, professionalism was a long time in coming. Since the war there have been two distinct periods – up to 1956, when regional leagues were played, using amateur players; and since that date, when the league has been dominated by Ajax of Amsterdam, and Feyenoord of Rotterdam – both of whom won the European Cup, the former on three successive occasions. Both win league games by, sometimes, very large margins; thereby allowing them to play with relaxation a system of 'total football'. Certainly, they were much favoured in the 1973 tournament, in which they sometimes played with breathtaking skill and poise; and in Johan Cruyff have a player of the highest talent, who together with Johan Neeskens, has taken his considerable skills from Holland to F.C. Barcelona in Spain.

World Cup achievement:

1934 – Lost in first round
1938 – Lost in first round
1950 – 1970 Did not qualify
1974 – Finalists

Hungary

The game was introduced here at the end of the last century, and the football association was formed in 1901, the year Hungary played its first international, losing 2-0 at home to Austria. But the game grew quickly, players of real skill – such as Schlosser and Orth – became world-famous for their skills with the football, and no one was much surprised when Hungary reached the Final of 1938. They were, however very surprised when the team manager dropped the combative Toldi and the eager, young Turai and chose instead two ball-playing 'stars' in Szucs and Vince. Italy won 4-2, and the whole of Hungary went into mourning.

The same happened in the 1954 World Cup, when Hungary arrived with a team packed with stars, still remembering their two victories over England of the previous months – by 7-1 and 6-3. They reached the Final, chose Puskas although he'd been injured and was still not 100 per cent fit and lost to West Germany by a scoreline of 3-2; although they'd trounced the Germans 8-3 in a group match!

Many of their leading players emigrated following the Communist take-over in 1956, and although Hungary has always had a good team there have been many disappointments on the football field in the last twenty or so years. But now they have a young side full of talent and impatient for success, who qualified at the expense first of Greece and Russia – and then of Bolivia.

World Cup achievement:

1930 – Did not enter
1934 – Beaten in Second Round
1938 – Finalists
1950 – Did not enter
1954 – Finalists
1958 – Eliminated by Wales in play-off for quarter-final place
1962 – Quarter-finalists
1966 – Quarter-finalists
1970 – Did not qualify
1974 – Did not qualify

Italy

Although the game was introduced by a Turin businessman, Eduardo Bosio (who had visited England and been taken by the game), Genoa Football and Cricket Club was the first of the great clubs; and English entrepreneurs had much to do with its growth.

But the key figure in the early years of the game in Italy was undoubtedly Vittorio Pozzo – who was in charge of the Italian team that played in the 1912 Olympiad in Stockholm; and who managed the professional team from 1929 to 1948, twice winning the World Cup.

Since the war the amount of paper-money attached to the game has grown rapidly, and the transfer fees allotted to players have grown crazy. But year in, year out the same four teams from Milan and Turin – A.C. Milan, Internazionale of Milan, Juventus and Torino – finish in top place; that monopoly having been broken five times, twice by Fiorentina, and once each by Bologna, Cagliari and the team from Rome, Lazio. But Italy has often been the leading country in Europe for the importation of players, and during the early Fifties the Italian league came close to resembling United Nations sub-committees.

Tactically shrewd, technically brilliant Italian players are fiercely drilled; but in Antognoni and Causio have midfield players of sheer class who play with flair almost everywhere they go and as a vast percentage of the population of Argentina is of Italian origin, they should receive a rapturous welcome.

World Cup achievement:

1934 – Winners
1938 – Winners
1950 – Second in group
1954 – Lost play-off for quarter-final place
1958 – Failed to qualify
1962 – Third in group
1966 – Third in group
1970 – Second
1974 – Third in group

World Cup 1970. Geoff Hurst's header just skimmed the post for what might have been the conclusive goal in the England–West Germany quarter-final. Schulz, Maier and Fichel are the German defenders.
United Press International

Above: World Cup 1970. Uwe Seeler (left) and Franz Beckenbauer after the latter had scored the first West German goal in England's 3–2 quarter-final defeat. Seeler also played in the tournaments of 1958, 1962 and 1966. For Beckenbauer, one of the world's most majestic players, the 1974 tournament was his third. *United Press International*

Right: World Cup 1970. Gerd Muller, who would be the tournament's highest scorer, here slashes the ball past Bonetti for his side's victorious goal in the quarter-final tie against England. Prowling nearby is the English captain, Bobby Moore.
Syndication International

Le Roy
DA EN TODO MEXIC
PHILCO
EXCELSIO
PARA TODA LA FAMILIA
ISRAEL

Left: World Cup 1970. Gianni Rivera (not in picture) scores the decisive goal in the Italy–West Germany semi-final. In picture, from left: Riva, Maier, Vogts, Schnellinger, Schulz (on ground), Boninsegna. *United Press International*

Above: World Cup 1970. Brazil's central spearhead in their victorious team – Tostao, Pelé, Jairzinho. *Syndication International*

Left: World Cup 1970. A scene from the final, won by Brazil over Italy 4–1. Jairzinho (Brazil) by-passing the attentions of Facchetti (Italy) while Burgnich (Italy), Pelé (Brazil) and De Sisti (Italy) look on. In the background is Mazzola.

Syndication International

Above: World Cup 1970. Jairzinho (right) moments after he had scored Brazil's third goal in the final against Italy. Facchetti is the tall defender, Albertosi the beaten goalkeeper.

United Press International

Above: World Cup 1974. Australian goalkeeper Reilly punches clear from East German forward Vogel. *Sport & General*

Right: World Cup 1974. Denis Law gets in a shot for Scotland in the opening match against Zaire, despite the attentions of Mwepu and Bwanga. Peter Lorimer looks on. *Sport & General*

LEOPARDS
ZAÏRE

Right: World Cup 1974. Julio Montero Castillo (Uruguay) looks amazed to be shown the red card that will send him off the field, in the opening match against Holland.

Popperfoto

Below: World Cup 1974. Suurbier (Holland) prevents a header from Pedro Rocha from going into the Dutch goal.

Popperfoto

Above: World Cup 1974. Bremner's face tells the story, as he watches his shot skimming past the Brazil post – on the wrong side! Leao is the beaten keeper, Hay and Piazza the other players.
Popperfoto

Right: World Cup 1974. Two heads going up simultaneously: that of Sandy Jardine in the defence for Scotland being unable to prevent that of Karasi, the substitute for Yugoslavia, from scoring the opening goal.
Popperfoto

ethmann Bank
mints

Left: World Cup 1974. All-out action from the game between Italy and Poland. The Polish players are in the light shirts and the line-up reads Lato, Facchetti, Szarmach and Morini.

Sport & General

Above: World Cup 1974. Muller (West Germany) tries to win the ball while 'sandwiched' between two defenders from Holland (Suurbier and Rijsbergen) in the Final.

Popperfoto

World Cup 1974. The winning side from West Germany. Top row, left to right: Decker, Hottges, Maier, Flohe, Muller, Grabowski, Breitner, Schwarzenbeck and Cullman. Bottom row, left to right: Nigbur, Hoeness, Heynckes, Bonhof, manager Helmut Schoen, Beckenbauer (with new World Cup), Holzenbein, Vogts and Overath.

Sport & General

Northern Ireland

In sports such as golf, amateur boxing, show-jumping, Rugby Union football and others, teams represent the whole of Ireland; in football – no. For many years in between the wars, a system was arranged whereby players from the North and South came together to play the most important matches. But since this ceased to function in 1950 Ireland has had two teams in the World Cup, the European Nations Championship and the European club competitions. The two teams have seen many players of genius, such as George Best, but only on one occasion has a team from Northern Ireland qualified through to play in a Final tournament – and that in 1958, when the team was managed by that famous inside-forward Peter Doherty.

They won through to a play-off match with Czechoslovakia, goal-difference not being recognised in those days; and their team which contained Gregg, the brothers Blanchflower, Peacock, Cush, the young Derek Dougan, McIlroy and McParland, a depleted team from Northern Ireland beat Czechoslovakia 2-1 to qualify for the quarter-finals – in which a depleted team lost to France 4-0, three goals coming in the second half.

Now managed by Danny Blanchflower, they achieved a remarkable result in their qualifying group by going to play Holland in Rotterdam and coming away with a draw.

Peru

With a football association founded in 1922 Peru has always lived with the problem of having its better players being drawn to play abroad. A team representing Peru took part in the first World Cup of 1930 in which it lost both its games, the second by the only score of the match to Uruguay, the eventual winners. Their next appearance in a World Cup was in 1970 and with a team assembled and coached by Didì the ex-star of the midfield for Brazil that gave a vast amount of pleasure to a world-wide audience by its spirited running from defence into attack. The present team seems to be made up of a mixture of old stars from 1970 – such as Chumpitaz, Sotil and Cubillas; and new talent such as Velasquez, a goal-scoring midfield player and Munante and Oblitas who are fast-running wingers capable of making quick incursions in attack.

Poland

Founded in 1923, the game in Poland was at first much influenced by the Hungarians; who sent coaches into Poland and encouraged the Polish players to go to Budapest to learn new systems and styles of play. They learnt the game so quickly that they sent a team to the World Cup of 1938; when they lost their opening game to Brazil 6-5, with a period of extra time. Their blond inside-forward, Willimowski, scored twice before extra time, twice during it and must have been very peeved to have scored four goals and still finish on a losing side!

Another thirty-five years were to pass before Poland made their next appearance in a World Cup final tournament: and they pleased many people with their displays of cunning, fast football during the 1974 World Cup. Two years previously, they had won the Olympic Games football tournament – which gave some warning as to what they might achieve later. To reach that tournament they beat out England – winners in 1966, one of the best two or three teams in Mexico four years later. They seemed to have a goalkeeper of skill, bravery and undoubted good fortune in Tomaszewski, who seemed to be all arms and legs when Poland met England at Wembley, blocking everything – and there was much – that came his way. In the tournament proper they had the most assured player in midfield in Deyna; in attack the darting performances of Lato went some way to making up for the absence through injury of the very skilled and forceful striker, Lubanski; Gorgon was a master in the heart of the defence; and the whole team played with an enthusiasm that was captivating. Of course, there have been changes in the team but we are sure to see much gusto and exuberance in Argentina in the next summer.

World Cup achievement:

1938 – Knocked out in first round

1950 – 1970 Did not qualify

1974 – Third

Scotland

After England's, the oldest association in the world, founded in 1873. It was in Scotland that the art of teamwork first came to be perfected – for south of the border, players were still far too keen to run with the ball themselves. Thus was born the Scottish 'school' of football, with its accent on quick-passing movements; and the tradition has come down over the decades, throwing up a myriad of fine players who play in the 'thinking' positions.

Given its talent for breeding players of skill, Scottish football has suffered cruelly at two points – through bad administration, and through the fact that many leading players have been transferred to play south by the use of English money. This last fact has made it a bit difficult for international teams to play at full strength and benefit from sessions of squad training.

Everyone was agreed that Scotland were very unfortunate not to go forward from their group in the 1974 World Cup; and much admired their nerve and drive in the games they played, with the play of their captain – Billy Bremner – much praised.

Like all the countries in Britain, Scotland stayed out of FIFA until 1946.

World Cup achievement:

1950 – Refused to compete
1954 – Last in qualifying group
1958 – Last in qualifying group
1962 – Failed to qualify
1966 – Failed to qualify
1970 – Failed to qualify
1974 – Third in qualifying group, went out on goal difference

Sweden

Sweden was one of the first Continental countries to adopt soccer as a game. As early as 1908, the Swedes entered a team for the Olympic Games. Sweden competed in both the World Cups of 1934 and 1938: and since the war they have made appearances in the World Cup finals in 1950, 1958 (when they were the host Country and finished as Finalists), 1970 and 1974.

In 1948 they won the Olympic soccer tournament and after they had finished in the final pool of the 1950 tournament, Italian clubs reached for their cheque-books. Of the players who went to play in Italy the most illustrious were the three Nordahl brothers, Gunner Gren, Nils Liedholm and Kurre Hamrin – an outside-right of verve and dazzling skills.

It was a small Yorkshireman, George Raynor, who began the process of making Sweden a powerful footballing nation in the years just after the war. And the systems he began to teach seem to have found good players – even in these times with Ove Kindvall a few years ago – a central striker of great ability, Ronnie Hellstroem – a goalkeeper who plays with great courage and some skill and Rald Edstroem, an attacker of great height and some verve.

World Cup achievement:

1930 – Did not enter
1934 – Beaten in second round
1938 – Quarter-finalists
1950 – Semi-finalists, fourth
1954 – Failed to qualify
1958 – Finalists
1962 – Failed to qualify
1966 – Failed to qualify
1970 – Third in qualifying round
1974 – Second in qualifying round, third in group in second round

Wales

As with Northern Ireland, they have so far made only the one appearance – and at the same tournament – the World Cup of 1958. They got there by a curious route: when all the teams drawn to play Israel withdrew FIFA decreed that all the teams to finish second should have their names drawn from a hat, that team to play Israel. In due course Wales beat Israel: and played in the final tournament with a brave and skilled goalkeeper in Kelsey, an inside-forward of special gifts in Ivor Allchurch and a powerful and effective centre-forward in John Charles – who had been displaying his strengths on behalf of the Italian side of Juventus. In the event he would miss the crucial quarter-final tie against Brazil, out through injury; but all the Welsh team played heroically, and Brazil only won through a goal that Pelé later described as being the most important of his life.

The present team, managed by Mike Smith, makes up for lack of pure skill with gusto, energy and competitiveness. In James they have a winger of some class and in Yorath a player of some determination. They were the only British team to feature in the later stages of the 1976 European Nations Championship; and in this tournament recorded a convincing win against Czechoslovakia – who were thought by many people to be one of the most powerful sides in the world.

West Germany

Football there began at the end of the last century, in the universities, and was much encouraged by local entrepreneurs. The association was founded in 1900, the game grew quickly, and by the time the World Cup competition began, the team from Germany was a force very much to be reckoned with. It has been since the war, however, that their game has been most impressive. Under the wily manager Sepp Herberger, the team from West Germany won the World Cup in 1954.

And under Helmut Schoen (who had served under Herberger for some time), came further triumphs. The performances of the national team over the past decade are most impressive and show that they have many good players, brilliant technique and tactics based on the very solid style of their play – which came to fruition in their victories in the 1974 World Cup and the 1972 European Nations Championship. They are reputed to have decreed against the sale of players abroad until after the next World Cup. They took a team to South America which proved to be vastly successful and proved that several new players had come into form at just the right time. They will be hard to beat in the summer of 1978.

World Cup achievement:

1934 – Semi-finalists, third
1938 – Beaten in first round
1950 – Barred from entry
1954 – Winners
1958 – Semi-finalists, fourth
1962 – Quarter-finalists
1966 – Finalists
1970 – Semi-finalists, third
1974 – Winners

These, then, are some of the teams who may shine in the 1978 tournament. And we may see a new system to follow the 4-4-2 or 4-3-3 or 1-4-3-2. But whatever the system let us all hope we see a championship that is positive – players of flair, ideas of attack that outweigh the systems of defence that some teams are bound to employ. And let's not forget that there are many examples of fine teams who have not won the World Cup, yet bequeathed to the memory of the tournament more than the victors. It's a truth worth remembering.

5 SOME OF THE WORLD'S LEADING PLAYERS

Few of these players come from England. From being the winners of the World Cup in 1966 and one of the two or three best teams in the trophy played for four years later, England failed to qualify for the tournament in 1974, leaving Scotland as the only British team to play in West Germany.

Our newspaper coverage of the game as played abroad, although getting better, is still pitifully inadequate; and so scant with information about teams who play abroad, as to be nearly insulting. Go to Italy, to Spain, to France and to Brazil and you will see coverage in daily papers of all sporting events that is much more thorough than our own, really 'world-wide'. And ask any Frenchman or Spaniard or Italian the most recent placings in the English First Division and he is very likely to know; but ask any Briton or Irishman to name the final placings in a recent paper and he will stare at you as though he thinks you have gone mad or will call you 'daft' – and walk quickly by!

So here, then, is a quick look at some of the world's top players – many of whom will be playing in the 1978 tournament:

Giancarlo ANTOGNONI (Italy). Born 1 April 1954. I was lucky enough to be in Florence when he made his home debut for Fiorentina at the end of October 1972, and saw at once that he was a player of extraordinary talent. He likes to use his skill especially to run long distances with the ball, beating player after player on the way. Deadly with free kicks, many of his scoring shots come from them. The Turin club of Juventus are said to have offered the equivalent of £1,500,000 in an unsuccessful bid to tempt him away.

Daniel BATHENAY (France). Powerful midfield player from

the club of St Etienne. Adept at running into positions from which he can use his strong shot to score goals.

Romeo BENETTI (Italy). Born 29 October 1945, a much-transferred midfield player, now with the champions of Italy Juventus of Turin. Full of hard running, he loves to build up attacks; as he did when Italy played England in November 1976 laying off a pinpoint cross from which Bettega scored. A rugged tackler, he played in the 1974 World Cup.

Roberto BETTEGA (Italy). Born 27 December 1950, his goal against England in their match in Rome was described by Bill Shankly (the former manager of Liverpool) as being 'the goal of the century' – a high, diving header that rocketed into the net after a crisp build-up. At the moment one of the best forwards in European football.

Rainer BONHOF (West Germany). Plays for his club, Borussia Moenchengladbach, as central defender but played a wonderful tournament in the 1974 World Cup in midfield. Very gifted in passing, he has a very wide vision of play.

Martin BUCHAN (Scotland). A centre-back of great poise, he played with great calmness and skill in the 1974 World Cup, having a brilliant game against Brazil where he helped to block the danger that might have come from Jairzinho.

Franco CAUSIO (Italy). Fast and clever, he caused havoc on the left side of England's defence when the countries first met in their qualifying group. Born 1 February 1949 he played in the 1974 tournament, and joined the Turin team of Juventus from the Sicilian team of Palermo. Widely regarded, with Antognoni, as one of the Italian players of great talent.

Antonio Carlos CEREZO (Brazil). The newest star of Brazil's midfield Toninho Cerezo is being compared by many observers to past stars such as Didì or Gerson. He can pass the ball vast distances with pinpoint accuracy and is lethal when shooting at goal.

Paulo CESAR (Brazil). Flamboyant, debonair midfield player who played as a reserve in 1970 and as first choice in 1974. Since Pelé's retirement has become a key figure in the side as being a player of high speed, superb dribbling ability and a deadly shot in either foot.

Mike CHANNON (England). Greatly feared in Europe for his powerful running with the ball and it is true that few players in the world are so dangerous as he when running at a defence. First capped at the end of 1972, he has been almost ever-present in England teams since then.

Hector CHUMPITAZ (Peru). An old favourite from the 1970 World Cup, solid in defence and useful in attack when moving forward from defence towards goal. Now in his middle thirties but still capable of some telling play in defence.

Ray CLEMENCE (England). Came to Liverpool – and won an England Under-23 cap before he gained a place in the Liverpool side! Tremendous concentration and quick reflexes have helped him to be considered among the best of goalkeepers.

Johan CRUYFF (Holland). Widely thought of as being one of the world's leading players, he is on record as not being keen to take part in this tournament. I wonder. Three times voted European Footballer of the Year – in 1971, 1973 and 1974 – he is a player of immense skills and speed. He made his debut for Ajax of Amsterdam in the 1965–66 season, and went on with them to lose one European Cup Final and win three others in 1971, 1972 and 1973. Suspended for a year for 'ungentlemanly conduct' early in his career he now plays for the Spanish club of F.C. Barcelona – along with his co-patriot, Johan Neeskens.

Teofilo CUBILLAS (Peru). Shone in the 1970 World Cup as a winger who became feared for his sinuous dribbling and fierce shooting. Said to be playing as well as ever now.

Kenny DALGLISH (Scotland). Played in his team's midfield during the 1974 tournament, always with a fair amount of skill and plenty of drive. He has played for Celtic in the past decade, and thus has much experience of the European club competitions.

Kazimierz DEYNA (Poland). A player of infinite guile and cunning, it was his superb passing that did much to open the door to his team's triumph in the 1974 trophy.

Dragan DZAJIC (Yugoslavia). Wing forward with sleight of foot leading to brilliant ball control, and deadly finishing, he played in the 1974 World Cup; and also the final tournaments of the European Nations Championships of 1968 and 1972.

Giacinto FACCHETTI (Italy). Played in the World Cups of 1966, 1970 and 1974 as a full-back but now plays as 'sweeper'. Born on 18 July 1942 this tall defender, six foot four inches, is a master at play that's normally economical.

Klaus FISCHER (West Germany). Central striker who scored seven goals in five appearances at the beginning of 1977. His eagerness to do well is heightened by the fact that he was found guilty of trying to 'fix' matches in the early 70s and banned from international football for some years.

Trevor FRANCIS (England). First capped in 1977 this exciting striker has for many seasons been astonishing crowds all over England with his skills on the ball. Played superbly against Brazil in the summer and then was amazingly dropped.

GIL (born as Gilberto Alves) (Brazil). Fast striker with a lethal shot in either foot and superb strength with his 'headers'. Part of the new wave of players from Brazil, he burst on to the international scene in 1975; and played many times for his country in 1976 – when it remained undefeated.

Francesco GRAZIANI (Italy). Central attacker, who finished as leading scorer in Italy in the 1976–77 season. He dovetails neatly with his colleague Bettega and must be considered to be one of the best finishers in Europe. Scored twice when England beat Italy in New York in May 1976.

Steve HEIGHWAY (Eire). This long-striding winger, loves to come in and cause havoc in the centre with his canny dribbling. Had a great season last winter, scoring goal after goal and wreaking worries in opposing defences.

Ronnie HELLSTROEM (Sweden). Played in the 1970 and 1974 World Cups, famous for his coolness and dexterity. He was only 21 in the 1970 World Cup, so should still be playing well into the '80s.

Bernd HOLZENBEIN (West Germany). Played in the 1974 World Cup team in attack making up for his lack of skill with youthful enthusiasm. With experience has come this skill and he now plays midfield for his country. Took part in the highly successful tour of South America in the summer of 1977 with wins against Uruguay 2-0, Argentina 3-1 and a 1-1 draw with Brazil.

Leighton JAMES (Wales). A winger of outstanding skill and real speed, with a liking for closing in, and shooting at, goal. First capped in 1971 and has been recently an almost ever-present. Inclined to be a bit moody.

Pat JENNINGS (Northern Ireland). Universally recognised as being one of the best goalkeepers in Europe, won first cap while still with Watford. Utterly fearless, he is full of spectacular saves near goal, and very agile excursions out of it.

Joe JORDAN (Scotland). Played in the 1974 World Cup with great flair, enthusiasm and courage. He has good close control on the ground and a fine use of his height to create danger from balls played with his head.

Kevin KEEGAN (England). Born 14 February 1951, this player has given vast pleasure to people all over Europe with his determined running in attack, weaving now this way, now that way. He has had much to do with the success of Liverpool in the first half of the '70s, and is widely thought of as being the most 'Latin' of English players.

Rudi KROL (Holland). Left-back who had a marvellous World Cup in 1974 playing well during all the successful Holland games. Strong in the tackle he likes to come forward and aid attacks.

Grzegorz LATO (Poland). Only came into the side following the injury to Lubanski, quickly earned a regular place and finished the 1974 World Cup as leading scorer. A winger full of dangerous running he climbs very high in the air for a comparatively short man.

Emerson LEAO (Brazil). Born 11 June 1949 he played in the 1974 World Cup and seems well on the way towards playing for Brazil for years to come.

Vladimierz LUBANSKI (Poland). Central attacker of great skill and courage he was put out of the game for a long time after receiving a 'rude' tackle by an English defender in June 1973. A lethal shot with either foot, he is also adept at scoring with his head; and now, thankfully, has resumed his career.

Danny McGRAIN (Scotland). As did Jordan, played in all Scotland's games in their luckless attempt on the 1974 World Cup. Clever at defending and most skilful at making runs of deep penetration down the right touchline, he sets up magnificent chances for his teammates.

Gordon McQUEEN (Scotland). Travelled to the 1974 World Cup, didn't play but since has become the team's centre-back, with a fine talent for using his height to play balls in the air in both defence and attack. A rugged tackler.

Sepp MAIER (West Germany). Played in the tournaments of 1970 and 1974 – in both of which he distinguished himself by his bravery and skill. Playing for Bayern Munich has given him a vastly successful career in European club football; and he has been very much part of his country's recent successes.

Francisco MARINHO (Brazil). This blond-haired fullback played a very conspicuous part in the 1974 World Cup, making one surging run into attack after another.

Marian MASNY (Czechoslovakia). Tricky winger, who created both goals in his country's victory over England in the qualifying round of the 1976 European Nations Championship – which his team finally won.

Don MASSON (Scotland). One of a clutch of midfield players – including Rioch, Hartford and the mercurial Gemmill – to be seen, and admired, in South America in the summer of 1977. He makes up for his lack of pace about the field by telling use of the ball. Good with free-kicks, he takes most of his side's penalties.

Dieter MULLER (West Germany). Like his famous namesake, Gerd, an attacker who likes to play at centre-forward – always searching for good openings to run into with speed. Had a fortunate introduction to international football in the 1976

European Nations Championship – when he scored against Yugoslavia with his first touch of the ball.

Johan NEESKENS (Holland). Really shone in the 1974 World Cup and scored many goals from penalties – including one early on in the Final, which was to prove futile. Followed Cruyff to play in Spain. He was a member of the Ajax of Amsterdam side which won the European Cup three years in succession in the early Seventies.

Tibor NYILASI (Hungary). A great goal-scoring central attacker, he burst on to the scene two years ago. Then he suffered a fracture of his skull, and though fully recovered now his progress has slowed.

Anton ONDRUS (Czechoslovakia). Tall, fair-haired centre-back who was absolutely authoritative in his country's victory in the 1976 European Nations Championship. Not surprisingly for a tall man, his play with the head is superb; and he is as well very intelligent. His play was one of the reasons that his country went unbeaten through a period of two years, from February 1975 onwards.

Luis PEREIRA (Brazil). Born 21 June 1949, he played in the 1974 World Cup; being sent off for committing a foul tackle on Neeskens. One of the best defenders in the world he has played much of his recent football in Spain.

Sandor PINTER (Hungary). A much-capped player in midfield, he runs all the time whether into defence or attack and fits into the team better every game. A goal-scorer, he makes his mark helping his colleagues to score as well by providing some great crosses from either wing.

Michel PLATINI (France). The best player in France since the legendary Raymond Kopa. Always full of enthusiasm, whether advancing from midfield or in attack, he has abundant skill and a great deal of resolution. He seems to have also the nice habit of being in the right place at the right time – to score goals.

Robert RENSENBRINK (Holland). Played in the 1974 World Cup and 1976 European Nations Championship being a winger of speed and skill, and a remarkable dribbler and scorer.

Roberto RIVELINO (Brazil). Came on to the international scene in 1968 when he toured Europe with a Brazilian team. Played in the 1970 and 1974 World Cups showing many talents and a sharpness at deadball situations. Now it might be said that the Brazil team is built round his talents and he uses his great skills at passing the ball accurately together with his thunderous shooting to pose threats to all defences.

ROBERTO (born as Carlos Roberto de Oliveira) (Brazil). A central attacker of great pace and skill who played three good games in the 1976 American Bicentennial tournament; scoring against Italy a goal that will long be remembered, beating one defender after another before putting past Zoff a fast rising shot.

Dominique ROCHETEAU (France). No one will forget the eight minutes he played for St Etienne in the European Cup Final of 1976 where he had far little time to show his amazing skills with the ball – both in wonderful dribbling and fierce shooting. Plays in attack for France and in the next World Cup will give great pleasure to many with his incisive play.

Karl-Heinz RUMMENIGGE (West Germany). An attacker of great flair, he burst on to the scene during the 1975–76 season, and played for Bayern Munich when the club won the European Cup for the third successive time. Inclined to be over-zealous to the point of being somewhat selfish.

Mario TARDELLI (Italy). Tends to play fullback for his country, and midfield for his club, Juventus. First capped in

April 1976, his powerful running forward and deceptive change of pace help to set up scoring chances for his colleagues.

Jan TOMASZEWSKI (Poland). Not many Englishmen will forget this player – who had such a successful night in goal when Poland kept England out of the 1974 World Cup. He went on to play most effectively in that tournament mixing his undoubted skill with a sense of sheer theatre.

John TOSHACK (Wales). Famed throughout Europe for his powerful play with the head, this tall striker won his first cap in 1969; and though he has been on the side-lines through injury, benefits very much from the high standard of the opposition he gets to play against for Liverpool.

Béla VARADI (Hungary). Fast-running, ball-playing left winger he has a fierce shot. Excellent in set pieces he has won many caps.

Bertie VOGTS (West Germany). A defender of real class Vogts did a marvellous job of man-to-man marking on Cruyff in the 1974 World Cup Final. Very mobile, he's not averse to running into forward positions to help the attack.

Terry YORATH (Wales). Showed in the past two seasons that he has gained so much from being reserve *de luxe* to those fine midfield players at Leeds United, Bremner and Giles. He has proved to be an excellent general for his country whether in defence or attack, and his charisma has been invaluable in making his country so successful during the past two seasons.

Renato ZACCARELLI (Italy). Forceful midfield player who likes to come forward fast from defence. Always worries the opposition by his forthright tackling, he scores fairly regularly as well.

ZICO (born as Artur Antunes Coimbra) (Brazil). A midfield player of great skill, he has a very wide vision of the pitch, likes to make passes of up to forty metres, and is always running forward to score goals. In fact in 1974 he finished the season as the top scorer in Brazil, and people thought he'd be another Tostao; but perhaps another Garrincha – with his magic dribbling – is more apposite.

Dino ZOFF (Italy). Born 28 February 1942, tall and courteous, he made appearances in the winning 1968 European Nations Championship and 1974 World Cup sides. Went 1,143 minutes without conceding a goal. Among the best goalkeepers in the world.

6 SOME STATISTICS

Number of Entries

1930 – 13
1934 – 29
1938 – 25
1950 – 29
1954 – 35
1958 – 51 (four countries withdrew without playing a game)
1962 – 56 (three countries withdrew without playing a game)
1966 – 53
1970 – 71
1974 – 94 (four countries withdrew without playing a game)
1978 – 103 (five countries withdrew without playing a game)

Attendances at Final matches

URUGUAY – 90,000 (Montevideo)
ITALY – 50,000 (Rome)
FRANCE – 45,000 (Paris)
BRAZIL – 200,000 (record) (Rio de Janeiro)
SWITZERLAND – 60,000 (Berne)
SWEDEN – 50,000 (Stockholm)
CHILE – 70,000 (Santiago)
ENGLAND – 100,000 (Wembley Stadium, London)
MEXICO – 112,000 (Mexico City)
WEST GERMANY – 80,000 (Munich)

Use of Players

Brazil hold the record for least players used by a World Cup winning team. In 1962 they needed only twelve players for their successful side: Gilmar, Santos (D), Santos (N), Mauro, Zizimo, Zito, Vavà, Didì, Garrincha and Zagalo – who played in all six matches; Pelé, who played in two; and Amarildo, who played in four.

Other winners, with the number of players used as follows:

1930 URUGUAY – 16
1934 ITALY – 17
1938 ITALY – 14
1950 URUGUAY – 14
1954 WEST GERMANY – 19
1958 BRAZIL – 16
1966 ENGLAND – 15 (Callaghan, Connelly, Greaves and Paine in addition to the winning team)
1970 BRAZIL – 14
1974 WEST GERMANY – 17

Leading Scorers

1930 STABILE (Argentine) 8
CEA (Uruguay) 5

1934 SCHIAVIO (Italy) 4
CONEN (Germany) 4
NEJEDLY (Czechoslovakia) 4

1938 LEONIDAS (Brazil) 8
SZENGELLER (Hungary) 7
PIOLA (Italy) 5

1950 ADEMIR (Brazil) 7
SCHIAFFINO (Uruguay) 5
BASORA (Spain) 5

1954 KOCSIS (Hungary) 11
MORLOCK (West Germany) 6
PROBST (Austria) 6
HUGI (Switzerland) 5

1958 FONTAINE (France) 13
PELÉ (Brazil) 6
RAHN (West Germany) 6
VAVÀ (Brazil) 5
McPARLAND (Northern Ireland) 5

1962 ALBERT (Hungary) 4
GARRINCHA (Brazil) 4
IVANOV (Russia) 4
JERKOVIC (Yugoslavia) 4
SANCHEZ (Chile) 4
VAVÀ (Brazil) 4

1966 EUSEBIO (Portugal) 9
HALLER (West Germany) 5
BENE (Hungary) 4
HURST (England) 4
PORKUJAN (Russia) 4
BECKENBAUER (West Germany) 4

1970 MULLER (West Germany) 10
JAIRZINHO (Brazil) 7*
CUBILLAS (Peru) 5
PELÉ (Brazil) 4
BISHOVETS (Russia) 4
** Jairzinho scored in each of the six rounds*

1974 LATO (Poland) 7
SZARMACH (Poland) 5
NEESKENS (Holland) 5
MULLER (West Germany) 4
REP (Holland) 4
EDSTROEM (Sweden) 4

Other goal-scoring statistics go like this: Hurst (England) remains the only man to score a hat-trick in a Final. The highest individual scoring feat in any game from the final grouping is four. Eight players have achieved this: Wetterstroem (Sweden v Cuba) 1938: Leonidas (Brazil v Poland) 1938: Willimowski (Poland v Brazil) 1938: Ademir (Brazil v Sweden) 1950: Schiaffino (Uruguay v Bolivia) 1950: Kocsis (Hungary v West Germany) 1954: Fontaine (France v West Germany) 1958: and Eusebio (Portugal v North Korea) 1966.

Placed together the best individual goal-scoring performances in the World Cup final tournaments go like this:

13 Fontaine 1958
11 Kocsis 1954
10 Muller 1970
9 Eusebio 1966
8 Stabile 1938
Leonidas 1938
7 Szengeller 1938
Ademir 1950
Jairzinho 1970
Lato 1974
6 Probst 1954
Morlock 1954
Pelé 1958
Rahn 1958

Total Number of Goals Scored in World Cup Final Stages

1930: 70 goals in 18 matches (3.8 per match)
1934: 70 goals in 17 matches (4.1 per match)
1938: 84 goals in 17 matches (4.6 per match)
1950: 88 goals in 22 matches (4.0 per match)
1954: 140 goals in 26 matches (5.3 per match)
1958: 126 goals in 35 matches (3.6 per match)
1962: 89 goals in 32 matches (2.7 per match)
1966: 89 goals in 32 matches (2.7 per match)
1970: 95 goals in 32 matches (2.9 per match)
1974: 97 goals in 38 matches (2.5 per match)

948 goals have been scored in 270 matches in 10 Final tournaments for an overall average of 3.5 goals per match.

The Trophy

The Jules Rimet Trophy – won outright by the Brazilians in 1970 on account of their third victory – was designed by the French sculptor, Abel Lafleur, stood a foot high and weighed in the region of nine pounds of gold. The present trophy – competed for in 1974 for the first time and known as the FIFA World Cup – was designed by an Italian, Silvio Gazzaniga, cost £8,000, was made in eighteen-carat gold and weighs about ten pounds.

Only five countries have won the World Cup:

Brazil (1958, 1962 and 1970),
Italy (1934 and 1938),
Uruguay (1930 and 1950),
West Germany (1954 and 1974)
and England (1966)

7 ARGENTINA AND THE WORLD CUP OF 1978

Football from Argentina has had, more than in many countries, a schizophrenic quality. The harsh, uncompromising quality is conjured up by the names of Juan Carlos Lorenzo – who managed the team that took part in the 1966 Final tournament – and that of Helenio Herrera – who took his teams at Internazionale of Milan through several years of dour play to win almost everything in sight; Antonio Rattin, sent off the field 'for the look on his face' when England played Argentina in 1966; and by the team of Estudiantes de la Plata, who played with overwhelming cynicism first against Manchester United, then against A.C.

Milan in the Intercontinental Trophy – and brought about sheer disgust and amazement in the local authorities, a massive feeling of guilt.

On the other side of the coin you have players from Argentina who brought their skills to Europe. Players such as the great di Stephano who was a deep-lying centre-forward of great skills and panache, one of the stars of the great side of Real Madrid in the late Fifties, and twice voted European Footballer of the Year. And the great player who went to Italy and played for Juventus of Turin – Omar Sivori, always breath-takingly sharp and positive when in front of goal; and now the national team manager, César-Luis Menotti, who believes that the team should develop its play through quickness and guile, and not through strength and toughness – this despite the fact that his side may play with one or two players called Killer!

The interest in football is large, noisy and very well-informed. They can be guaranteed to will their team forward, partly through the plain will to win, and partly because their performance in the World Cup tournaments so far (see the table in the next chapter) is a bit sad. One of the perennial problems has been lack of money, which has forced clubs to sell their best players to European football. In Spain there is one Killer, along with Kempes, Brindisi, Scotta, Cano and Moreta; while in France are Bianchi, Curoni and Alonso. It is no surprise to find that many of these are forwards but Menotti is trying his best to build up a team of home-based players, who can gain by receiving his advice often. He has resigned once already when a couple of club sides refused to release players for training with his team, but was persuaded to change his mind. And has done much to convince the authorities in Argentina that no more players should be transferred to Europe until after the 1978 tournament.

When they play:

The tournament opens with a game on June 1 and closes with the Final on June 25. The match to decide third place will take place on June 24; and, as in 1974, the first two in each group will go forward to play in further groups. These matches will take place on June 14, 18 and 21.

The climate:

It will be mid-winter in Argentina during June, and the temperature (if normal) will be in about the region of 50°–60° Fahrenheit (say 12° – 18° Centrigrade) with some places being, of course, warmer than others.

Hours of play:

To ease the televising of the matches to Europe (where they will be able to be seen on the same day), we will have games that start at 2 pm (British time 6 pm) or 4.30 pm (British time 8.30). All those matches featuring the side representing Argentina will start at 7 pm (British time 11 pm).

Leading local players:

Carlos BABINGTON: Played in midfield for Argentina in the 1974 World Cup combining well with Houseman, particularly in the game against Italy. He has lately taken his talents to West Germany.

Angel BARGAS: Central defender who played in the 1974 World Cup having been previously sold to the French club of Nantes, recently French champions.

Daniel BERTONI: plays on the left wing for his club, Independiente, being fast and deft; born 21 March 1955.

Carlos BIANCHI: Fast-moving, thrustful player who is one of the most successful strikers playing in France – where for the past two seasons he has headed the list of goal scorers.

Hugo Orlando GATTI: colourful character with long hair hanging down to his shoulders. Has good technique and is fearless; plays for Boca Juniors.

Rene HOUSEMAN: played in 1974 tournament; smallish he's very active in midfield for Huracan. Born 19 July 1953.

Mario KEMPES: plays in Spain, sold there by Rosario Central. Also played in the 1974 tournament, being one of the country's best attackers. Menotti will be highly tempted to use him in the team.

Oswaldo PIAZZA: Long striding central defender whose good form has had much to do with the success of the French side of St Etienne. He is particularly able at coming forward to involve himself in midfield.

Alberto TARANTINI: born 3 December 1955, a midfield star who plays all over the field – being swift enough to cover back in defence and move forward in attack.

Ricardo VILLA: Born 18 August 1952 this midfield player has made a very noticeable impression on the team's play in front of goal.

Security:

This, of course, will be plentiful and powerful, as for every major sporting tournament in the world. But there is the added measure, that Argentina has not yet found a political stability; which means that the police-force and Army will be out in strength.

The Groups:

As in the 1974 tournament, teams will play in four groups, the first two teams from each group moving forward to play in two further groups. The draw to see which teams play in which groups is on 14 January 1978; remembering of course that two teams are already known – Argentina (who go through as hosts) are the first team in Group I; and West Germany (who qualify as Holders) are the sixth team, and play in group II.

The teams will play thus: Group I (including Argentina) will play in Buenos Aires and Mar del Plata.

Group II (including West Germany) will play at Buenos Aires, Rosario and Cordoba.

Group III will play in Buenos Aires and Mar del Plata.

Group IV will play at Cordoba and Mendoza.

The stadia

Six stadia will be used in five cities and towns. These are Buenos Aires (which has two) and Rosario – where the stadia have been modernised; Mar del Plata, Cordoba (the farthest northwards of the grounds) and Mendoza (the farthest eastwards of the grounds) – where new stadia have been built.

BUENOS AIRES: with nine million inhabitants and two stadia. the first and largest is the stadium of River Plate – which holds 100,000 spectators (36,000 seated), has room for 2,200 journalists and will see the opening match and the Final and the second, smaller, stadium is that where the club Velez Sarfizld play – which has been reduced in size over the years to hold 53,000 spectators (28,000 sitting).

ROSARIO: with one million inhabitants, it has a stadium to hold 58,000 spectators (25,000 seated) and one of its two club sides nurtured both Carnevali and Kempes of the team who played in the 1974 tournament.

MAR DEL PLATA: with 350,000 inhabitants has a newly-built stadium that holds 45,240 spectators (17,000 seated). The farthest south of the centres, the stadium will see six games.

CORDOBA: with 850,000 inhabitants, its newly-constructed stadium will contain 53,237 spectators (25,000 seated). The stadium is set to the north-west of the town, about ten miles out.

MENDOZA: with 750,000 inhabitants and an entirely new stadium that holds 50,000 spectators (28,000 seated) and is set among a forest of trees. Highest ground in this tournament; six matches to take place here.

Diego Lucero

The only journalist to have seen all ten World Cup final tournaments since the opening one of 1930.

Clearance

In November 1976 two representatives from FIFA inspected the six stadia and their nearby facilities; as a result of which a special meeting of FIFA was held in Buenos Aires, at which clearance was given for the 1978 tournament to be held in Argentina.

Moats around the pitches:

As in most stadia in South America, the pitches in use for this tournament will have wide and deep moats around them.

Referees:

These will probably stay in Buenos Aires; and to eliminate the risks of being approached with offers of bribery, they will be flown out on very short notice to the matches they have been assigned to take charge of.

Why the Argentina team should do well:

Just look at the benefits given in past tournaments by the side playing in front of its own crowd.

URUGUAY 1930 – Winners
ITALY 1934 – Winners
FRANCE 1938 – Beaten by eventual winners
BRAZIL 1950 – Second
SWITZERLAND 1954 – Quarter-finalists
SWEDEN 1958 – Finalists
CHILE 1962 – Semi-finalists
ENGLAND 1966 – Winners
MEXICO 1970 – Quarter-finalists
WEST GERMANY 1974 – Winners

The local team start their matches with this great in-built advantage: and it will be very surprising if their talented team doesn't do well in the tournament.

8 WORLD CUP – FINAL SERIES 1930–1974 LEAGUE TABLE

		P	W	D	L	F	A
1	BRAZIL	45	29	7	9	109	53
2	WEST GERMANY	41	27	5	9	100	63
3	ITALY	29	16	5	8	53	34
4	URUGUAY	29	14	5	10	57	39
5	HUNGARY	23	13	2	8	70	34
6	SWEDEN	25	11	5	9	47	43
7	ENGLAND	24	10	6	8	34	28
8	YUGOSLAVIA	25	11	3	11	45	34
9	RUSSIA	19	10	3	6	30	21
10	ARGENTINA	22	9	4	9	40	39
11	CZECHOSLOVAKIA	22	8	3	11	32	36
12	CHILE	18	7	3	8	23	24
13	FRANCE	17	7	1	9	38	33
14	SPAIN	15	6	2	7	20	23
15	AUSTRIA	12	6	1	5	26	26
16	POLAND	8	6	0	2	21	11
17	SWITZERLAND	18	5	2	11	28	44
18	HOLLAND	9	5	1	3	17	9
19	PORTUGAL	6	5	0	1	17	8
20	MEXICO	21	3	4	14	19	50
21	EAST GERMANY	7	2	2	3	5	5
22	PARAGUAY	7	2	2	3	12	19
23	UNITED STATES	7	3	0	4	12	21
24	WALES	5	1	3	1	4	4
25	NORTHERN IRELAND	5	2	1	2	6	10
26	RUMANIA	8	2	1	5	12	17
27	SCOTLAND	8	1	3	4	7	15
28	PERU	6	2	0	4	10	13
29	BULGARIA	12	0	4	8	9	29
30	CUBA	3	1	1	1	5	12

Note well the lowly positions of both Holland and Poland – second and third in the 1974 tournament, which was for each of them the first post-war qualifying competition. And that, of course, of Portugal who have so far played in one final tournament – that of 1966. Much more may be heard of these teams in years to come; and their positions on this 'league' table will rise accordingly.